NATURALIZATIONS

OF

MEXICAN AMERICANS

Extracts
Volume 4

John P. Schmal

HERITAGE BOOKS
2007

HERITAGE BOOKS

AN IMPRINT OF HERITAGE BOOKS, INC.

Books, CDs, and more—Worldwide

For our listing of thousands of titles see our website
at
www.HeritageBooks.com

Published 2007 by
HERITAGE BOOKS, INC.
Publishing Division
65 East Main Street
Westminster, Maryland 21157-5026

International Standard Book Number: 978-0-7884-4283-4

TABLE OF CONTENTS

INTRODUCTION

Naturalizations of Mexican Americans: Extracts – Volume IV is a collection of 265 naturalization extracts, compiled from a period of several decades and across several American states. Since 1848, Mexican immigrants have been crossing the southern border to find employment and to escape from political turmoil. Although some of the immigrants returned to Mexico, many of them decided to stay in the United States and become American citizens.

When the descendants of these early immigrants try to research their family origins, they sometimes have problems locating information on their distant long-gone ancestors. After the passage of time and several generations, the birthplace of an ancestor may pass into legend. But locating the place of origin of an immigrant ancestor is essential to successful research and, for some ancestors, the only place to find this information may be naturalization records.

This collection of extracts – the fourth in a series – helps to remedy this problem by showing extracts from many naturalizations of Mexican Americans that took place for persons who have long since died. Seventy-six of the people

INTRODUCTION

profiled in these extracts were born between 1816 and 1870, 83 were born between 1871 and 1899, and the remaining 96 were born between 1901 and 1923.

Forty of the declarants and petitioners testified in their declarations or petitions that they had crossed the border between 1848 and 1880, and another 65 crossed between 1881 and 1900, at a time when no border crossing records were being kept. Ninety-two individuals crossed the border between 1900 and 1920, while the rest crossed the border between 1921 and 1945.

Mexico is a big country and, as a result, Mexican nationals seeking citizenship in the U.S. have traditionally hailed from many states. In the early Twentieth Century, many Mexican immigrants came from Sonora, Chihuahua, Coahuila, Guanajuato, Aguascalientes, Jalisco, and Zacatecas. Travel from the first three states was relatively easy because those states share their northern borders with the U.S. But travel from the other four states was made possible by Mexico's rapidly growing railroad system.

INTRODUCTION

The above-mentioned states are also the primary birth places of the declarants and petitioners in this volume. The primary states of origin for these citizenship candidates were: Coahuila (44), Nuevo Leon (36), Chihuahua (32), Jalisco (23), Sonora (18), Guanajuato (18), Zacatecas (16), Tamaulipas (14), and Durango (9). A significant number of persons also arrived from Mexico City and the states of Durango and Aguascalientes, among others.

Naturalizations after 1907 provide valuable information not only for the person seeking citizenship but also for their spouses. The extracts that we have compiled include many married individuals, so many of these extracts give a fair amount of information about the spouse as well, including their date and place of birth.

These extracts contain varying amounts of information on 100 spouses coming from a variety of places. More than one-quarter of the spouses of the citizenship candidates were born in the U.S., including Texas (9 spouses), Arizona (7), Kansas (5), California and Colorado. Several spouses also came from Italy and Peru. However, the lion's share of

INTRODUCTION

spouses were natives of Mexico, primarily from the States of Chihuahua (14 spouses), Jalisco (10), Guanajuato (8), Sonora (7), as well as Michoacán, Zacatecas, Aguascalientes and Mexico City.

Both *Declarations of Intentions* and *Petitions for Naturalization* have been included in this collection. For that reason, it is possible that some of the petitioners who filed Declarations of Intention may have not followed up with a Petition and thus did not actually achieve citizenship.

The naturalization extracts have been compiled from independent research undertaken by the author and from public records of the **National Archives and Records Administration (NARA).** Seventy-seven of these naturalizations took place in Arizona, Kansas or Colorado.

Although the Texas court records between 1884 and 1906 have considerable less content than the post-1907 naturalization records, they nevertheless may provide a link for the Mexican-American family historian seeking to find a place of origin for his or her ancestors in Mexico. One

INTRODUCTION

hundred and four records from the Maverick and Webb County courts in Texas have also been included because many of them contain valuable information relating to a place of birth for Mexican Americans who are, in some cases, five or six generations removed from the present generation. The rest of the declarations – numbering eighty-four – were filed in California courts.

Although Mexican Americans may have crossed the border in at least two dozen locations in the last century, El Paso was, by far, the port of entry most used. Ninety-four individuals in these extracts stated that they came to the United States through the El Paso Port of Entry.

Another sixty-nine individuals crossed at the Laredo Port of Entry in Texas. Thirty-six petitioners also came through the Eagle Pass Port of Entry. Significant numbers of these petitioners also used the Nogales, Naco and Douglas ports in Arizona, the San Ysidro and Calexico ports in California and the Roma and Brownsville ports in Texas.

INTRODUCTION

The extracts presented in this fourth volume are designed to provide the family history researcher with a link to their distant past. For naturalizations that took place after 1907, it is recommended, however, that the reader should contact NARA to get a full "Naturalization Certificate File (C-File)," which should usually consist of a Declaration of Intention, a Petition of Naturalization and a Certificate of Arrival.

Additionally, many NARA records have been filmed by the Family History Library in Salt Lake City and are available through the resources of local Family History Centers. Individuals who would like to pursue this option should use the "Place Search" at the following link:

http://www.familysearch.org/Eng/Library/FHLC/frameset_f hlc.asp

The reader should enter the name of the relevant county or state, and search for the category "Naturalization and citizenship." Microfilms located in this manner can be ordered from the Family History Library in Salt Lake City

INTRODUCTION

and be lent to local Family History Centers around the country for research.

GUIDE TO EXTRACTS

This chapter has been designed to provide the reader with a guide to understanding the information given in the extracts contained in this book. The information provided in naturalization documents changed over the decades, so there may appear to be some inconsistency in the extracts, due in large part to the fact that the naturalization documents span more than half a century and utilized several formats between the 1880s and the 1950s.

It is recommended that the reader who finds his or her ancestor mentioned in these extracts contact the local NARA facility to obtain all documents associated with the naturalization. If the extract is for a person making a declaration of intent in Maverick or Webb counties, Texas, the reader will want to contact the county clerk of the appropriate county. However, most of the naturalizations filed in county clerk offices before 1907 have very little detailed information on individuals. The author has copies of many – but not all – of the extracted documents.

1

GUIDE TO EXTRACTS

Name

This field provides the name of the petitioner. Sometimes two names are provided (an alias).

District Court

This field will give the name of the District or County Court, at which the Declaration of Intention or Petition for Naturalization was filed. The extracted records were on file in many district courts.

Address

The Address Field usually gives the street address of the applicant. In some places, a rural address or post office box has been provided.

Type of Record

The primary designations are Declaration of Intention and Petition for Naturalization.

DOB

DOB stands for "Date of Birth." Most often, an exact date of birth is given. For some persons, only a year has been

GUIDE TO EXTRACTS

indicated. For older county records, such as those in Webb and Bexar counties (Texas), a date of birth may not be provided, but the age of the applicant is given in parenthesis.

Place

The Place format generally provides a Mexican city and state, such as "Monterrey, Nuevo Leon" or "Teocaltiche, Jalisco." However, some people may have given only a state of birth, such as "Zacatecas, Mexico" which may indicate that the birthplace is in the City of Zacatecas or in the State of Zacatecas.

Another common place given in naturalization is "Chihuahua, Mexico." In most cases, this would indicate the City of Chihuahua in the State of Chihuahua, but it may also indicate that the petitioner simply came from somewhere in the State of Chihuahua. Similarly, "Aguascalientes, Mexico" probably refers to a native of the City of Aguascalientes in the State of Aguascalientes, but may also refer to a native of the state itself.

3

GUIDE TO EXTRACTS

It is up to the reader to interpret the correctness of such information. It is likely that the names of some cities have been misspelled. The author has made some spelling corrections.

Last Foreign Residence

Last Foreign Residence was commonly provided in the naturalization records after 1906. This represents an added aide to genealogical research, helping the researcher to reconstruct the immigrant's journey to America and indicating a place of residence in Mexico other than the petitioner's place of birth. The immigrant, in fact, may have married or had children in that location before actually crossing the border.

Married to

Early naturalization records did not ask for the names of spouses. Later naturalization records, however, did ask for a spouse's name, and eventually more detailed information, including a place and date of marriage, and a listing of their children and their children's dates of birth. Usually only a

GUIDE TO EXTRACTS

first name is given, in which case the reader should assume that the last names of the two spouses are identical.

Date

When available, a date of marriage is provided.

Where

When available, a place of marriage is provided. In many records, extensive information is provided on the spouse of the petitioner. In order to provide the maximum amount of information, such spousal information has been included, but is contained within parenthesis. The following are two examples of the format used to provide additional spousal information:

(Luz was born at Leon, Guanajuato, on June 15, 1898. She entered the U.S. at Laredo, Texas, in October 1916.)

(Manuel was born at Guadalajara, Jalisco, on Sept. 21, 1892. He entered the U.S. at El Paso, Texas, in November 1908.)

Crossed the Border on

This is the lawful date on which entry into the United States took place. In older records, it may only be given as a year.

GUIDE TO EXTRACTS

A woman who was married in the U.S. may have undergone a name change. In the extracts, the name used at the time of the crossing is sometimes indicated in parenthesis when it is different from the name at the top of the page.

An immigrant may have crossed the border several times before settling in the U.S. Naturalization forms ask for the final date of entry into the U.S.

Where

This field provides the port of entry of the immigrant.

Mode of travel

The Mode of Travel may include "on foot," "by railroad," by ship, or may specify a particular railroad. At the port of El Paso, the Mexican Central Railroad and the El Paso Electric Railway are frequently given as the means by which the petitioner crossed the border. At the Nogales, Arizona, Port of Entry, the Southern Pacific of Mexico Railway is frequently named.

GUIDE TO EXTRACTS

Date Certificate Issued

If readable and if available, the date of the document is provided. If possible, an earlier Declaration of Intention or a later Petition for Naturalization may be cited in parenthesis.

Alien Registration

In some later naturalization records, the alien registration number was provided. Such information provides the researcher with a secondary source of information to utilize.

Description

The naturalization records used after 1906 usually provided a very detailed physical description of the petitioner. Although the format varied over the years, the following example is one of the formats utilized:

Occupation: Laborer. Dark Complexion, 5 Feet, 6 Inches, 155 Pounds, Black Hair, Brown Eyes. Four children listed – all born between 1915 and 1924.

MEXICAN NATURALIZATIONS (1936-2004)

Mexican Naturalizations in the Pre-War Era

In the year 1936, 141,265 aliens were naturalized as American citizens. Of this number, only 623 citizens of Mexico renounced their allegiance to the Mexican Republic to become American citizens, representing only 0.44% of the total number of naturalized citizens during that year. In contrast, the following countries made the largest contribution to persons naturalized as American citizens:

1. The British Empire (42,231)
2. Germany (19,622)
3. Italy (17,781)
4. Poland (14,745)
5. The Soviet Union (3,525).

The coming of war to Europe during 1939 to 1940 led to increased immigration from European nations and it was these aliens who were most likely to seek naturalization. During this pre-war era, Mexican naturalizations increased, but not on the same level as European petitions for citizenship.

MEXICAN NATURALIZATIONS (1936-2004)

The Alien Registration Program

By 1940, the number of Mexicans who were naturalized rose slightly to 2,669, or 1.13% of all naturalizations. In contrast, a large number of Mexicans had registered as aliens. In response to the threat of war, the United States had launched the Alien Registration Program in July of 1940. Pursuant to the Alien Registration Act of that year, every alien resident in the United States had to register at their local Post Office while aliens entering the country registered as they applied for admission. Alien Registration requirements applied to all aliens over the age of fourteen, regardless of nationality and regardless of immigration status. As of December 31, 1940, 423,519 aliens from Mexico were registered under the Alien Registration Act.

In 1940, the nations contributing the most naturalized Americans were:

1. The British Empire (59,680)
2. Italy (37,357)
3. Poland (26,964)
4. Germany (25,802)
5. Soviet Union (15,598).

MEXICAN NATURALIZATIONS (1936-2004)

Mexican Naturalizations (1936-1950)

Below is a table indicating the number of Mexicans who were naturalized in each year from 1936 to 1950. The three peak years for naturalizations were war years (1943, 1944, 1945), after which naturalizations of Mexican nationals decreased dramatically.

Year	Mexican Aliens Naturalized	Mexican Aliens Naturalized as a Percentage of the Total	Total Persons Naturalized in the United States
1936	623	0.44%	141,265
1937	903	0.55%	164,976
1938	1,082	0.67%	162,078
1939	1,643	0.87%	188,813
1940	2,669	1.13%	235,260
1941	3,757	1.35%	277,294
1942	4,300	1.59%	270,364
1943	6,799	2.13%	318,933
1944	7,474	1.69%	441,979
1945	6,352	2.75%	231,402

11

MEXICAN NATURALIZATIONS (1936-2004)

Year	Mexican Aliens Naturalized	Mexican Aliens Naturalized as a Percentage of the Total	Total Persons Naturalized in the United States
1946	5,135	3.42%	150,062
1947	3,336	3.55%	93,904
1948	1,895	2.70%	70,150
1949	2,227	3.34%	66,594
1950	2,323	3.50%	66,346

In 1950, the number of Mexicans seeking American citizenship remained relatively small, making up only 3.5% of all naturalizations. However, among all the contributing nations, Mexico was in seventh place as the native land of persons who were naturalized in that year:

1. British Empire (12,829)
2. Italy (8,301)
3. Germany (6,065)
4. Canada (5,882)
5. Poland (3,793)
6. Philippines (3,257)
7. Mexico (2,323)

MEXICAN NATURALIZATIONS (1936-2004)

Operation Wetback and the Braceros

During the following decade, Mexican naturalizations increased significantly. Part of this increase may have been the result of the Bracero Program, which brought many Mexicans into the country as guest workers. Some Braceros eventually became citizens.

Another factor in increased naturalizations may have been the Border Patrol's "Operation Wetback," which had commenced in June 1954. It is possible that some Mexican nationals became citizens as a means of avoiding deportation.

MEXICAN NATURALIZATIONS (1936-2004)

Mexican Naturalizations (1951-1960)

A table illustrating the Mexican naturalizations from 1951 to 1960 follows:

Year	Mexican Aliens Naturalized	Mexican Aliens Naturalized as a Percentage of the Total	Total Persons Naturalized in the United States
1951	1,969	3.60%	54,716
1952	2,496	2.82%	88,655
1953	2,728	3.96%	92,051
1954	3,710	2.09%	177,831
1955	10,166	4.85%	209,526
1956	6,958	4.77%	145,885
1957	5,541	4.01%	138,063
1958	5,042	4.21%	119,866
1959	5,147	4.95%	103,931
1960	5,913	4.95%	119,442

By 1960, the annual number of Mexicans receiving naturalization had more than doubled from a decade earlier.

MEXICAN NATURALIZATIONS (1936-2004)

In that year, the countries that contributed the most naturalized citizens to the U.S. were:

1. Germany (19,003)
2. Italy (14,560)
3. United Kingdom (11,303)
4. Canada (10,215)
5. Poland (8,021)
6. Mexico (5,913)
7. Japan (4,189)

Mexican Naturalizations (1961-1970)

From a peak of 10,166 in 1955, Mexican naturalizations dropped steadily to a low point of 5,080 in 1965. After 1961, the naturalization of Mexican nationals fluctuated between 5,000 and 6,195 for the rest of the decade. At the same time, large numbers of Cubans, fleeing the Communist regime of Fidel Castro, flocked to the United States, many of them seeking American citizenship. The tense situation surrounding Berlin and the general Cold War atmosphere also proved a stimulus for Germans and other Europeans seeking American citizenship.

15

MEXICAN NATURALIZATIONS (1936-2004)

The following table illustrates the naturalizations of Mexicans from 1961 to 1970:

Year	Mexican Aliens Naturalized	Mexican Aliens Naturalized as a Percentage of the Total	Total Persons Naturalized in the United States
1961	8,405	6.35%	132,450
1962	7,205	5.66%	127,307
1963	5,285	4.26%	124,178
1964	5,213	4.64%	112,234
1965	5,080	4.87%	104,299
1966	5,677	5.15%	103,059
1967	6,044	5.76%	104,902
1968	6,134	5.97%	102,726
1969	5,111	5.18%	98,709
1970	6,195	5.61%	110,399

MEXICAN NATURALIZATIONS (1936-2004)

In 1970, the number of Mexicans who received naturalization was 6,195. In that year, the countries that contributed the most naturalized citizens to the U.S. were:

1. Cuba (20,888)
2. Germany (10,067)
3. Italy (7,892)
4. United Kingdom (7,549)
5. Canada (6,387)
6. Mexico (6,195)
7. Philippines (5,669)
8. Poland (3,426)
9. China and Taiwan (3,090)
10. Greece (2,906)

Mexican Naturalizations (1971-1990)

During the 1970s and 1980s, Mexican naturalizations began a steady increase, as illustrated in the following table:

Year	Mexican Aliens Naturalized	Mexican Aliens Naturalized as a Percentage of the Total	Total Persons Naturalized in the United States
1971	6,361	5.87%	108,407
1972	5,850	5.03%	116,215

MEXICAN NATURALIZATIONS (1936-2004)

Year	Mexican Aliens Naturalized	Mexican Aliens Naturalized as a Percentage of the Total	Total Persons Naturalized in the United States
1973	5,507	4.56%	120,740
1974	5,206	3.96%	131,455
1975	5,781	4.08%	141,537
1976	5,602	3.93%	142,504
3rd Quarter, 1976	1,505	3.12%	48,218
1977	6,301	3.94%	159,873
1978	8,662	4.99%	173,535
1979	8,046	4.90%	164,150
1980	9,341	5.91%	157,938
1981	9,545	5.74%	166,317
1982	11,423	6.58%	173,688
1983	12,594	7.04%	178,948
1984	14,575	7.40%	197,023
1985	23,042	9.42%	244,717
1986	27,087	9.65%	280,623
1987	21,999	9.69%	227,008

MEXICAN NATURALIZATIONS (1936-2004)

Year	Mexican Aliens Naturalized	Mexican Aliens Naturalized as a Percentage of the Total	Total Persons Naturalized in the United States
1988	22,085	9.12%	242,063
1989	18,520	7.92%	233,777
1990	17,564	6.50%	270,101

The devaluation of the Mexican peso in 1982 and the Immigration Reform and Control Act Amnesty of 1986 played a significant role in the dramatic rise in Mexican naturalizations that started in 1982.

At this point, there was a very noticeable shift in the countries contributing new citizens to the U.S. Fewer Europeans were arriving in the U.S. and seeking naturalization, while large numbers of immigrants from Latin America, the Caribbean, and Asia were seeking citizenship.

19

MEXICAN NATURALIZATIONS (1936-2004)

In 1987, the countries contributing the largest numbers of immigrants were:

1. Mexico (27,807)
2. Vietnam (25,469)
3. Philippines (25,296)
4. Korea (14,233)
5. Cuba (13,818)
6. Mainland China (9,208)
7. India (8,659)
8. Soviet Union (7,276)
9. United Kingdom (7,102)
10. Jamaica (6,563)

Mexican Naturalizations (1991-2000)

During the 1990s, Mexican naturalizations increased even more dramatically, in large part because of the 1994 financial crisis in Mexico and the reaction to Proposition 187 in California. In addition, many of the people who were granted amnesty during the 1980s were getting ready to fulfill their final requirements for citizenship, leading to a steep increase of naturalization petitions during the mid-1990s.

MEXICAN NATURALIZATIONS (1936-2004)

Year	Mexican Aliens Naturalized	Mexican Aliens Naturalized as a Percentage of the Total	Total Persons Naturalized in the United States
1991	22,066	7.16%	308,058
1992	12,873	5.36%	240,252
1993	23,615	7.50%	314,681
1994	46,169	11.33%	407,398
1995	81,655	16.73%	488,088
1996	254,988	24.41%	1,044,689
1997	142,569	23.83%	598,225
1998	112,442	24.28%	463,060
1999	207,750	24.73%	839,944
2000	189,705	21.34%	888,788

In 1996, the leading-edge of legal residents who qualified for amnesties during the 1980s had now fulfilled their citizenship requirements and sought citizenship in their adopted country.

21

MEXICAN NATURALIZATIONS (1936-2004)

In 2000, the countries contributing the largest numbers of immigrants were:

1. Mexico (189,705)
2. Vietnam (55,934)
3. China (54,534)
4. Philippines (46,563)
5. India (42,198)
6. Dominican Republic (25,176)
7. El Salvador (24,073)
8. Korea (23,858)
9. Jamaica (22,567)
10. Ukraine (16,849)
11. Poland (16,405)
12. Russia (12,919)

Mexican Naturalizations (2001-2003)

The table on the following page illustrates Mexican immigration in 2001, 2002 and 2003, but also provides the total number of Mexican nationals who were naturalized from 1936 to 2003. With the increased pace of naturalizations in the later decades, Mexican aliens seeking citizenship had come to represent more than one-tenth of all immigrants.

MEXICAN NATURALIZATIONS (1936-2004)

Year	Mexican Aliens Naturalized	Mexican Aliens Naturalized as a Percentage of the Total	Total Persons Naturalized in the United States
2001	103,234	16.97%	608,205
2002	76,531	13.24%	573,708
2003	56,093	12.11%	463,204
Total Naturalizations, 1936-2003	1,736,823	10.76%	16,143,596

The naturalization statistics in this chapter have been extracted from Immigration and Naturalization and Homeland Securities Annual Statistical Reports between 1936 and 2003.

NATURALIZATION EXTRACTS

Name: Eutimio Pasos Acuna
District Court: Superior Court, Cochise County, State of Arizona **Address:** Fairbank, Arizona
Type of Record: Declaration of Intention, No. 92546
DOB: Dec. 24, 1874 **Place:** Alamos, Sonora
Last Foreign Residence: Sinraguipi, Mexico
Married to: N.A. **Date:** N.A.
Where: N.A.
Crossed the Border on: December 15, 1888
Where: Palamenas, Arizona **Mode of travel:** Horseback
Date Certificate Issued: Dec. 7, 1914
Alien Registration: N.A.
Description: Occupation: Farmer. Dark Complexion, 5 Feet, 11 Inches, 160 Pounds, Black Hair, Brown Eyes.

NATURALIZATION EXTRACTS

Name: Sebastian Contreras Adame, Jr.
District Court: District Court, Topeka, Kansas
Address: 231 Adams, Topeka, Kansas
Type of Record: Petition for Naturalization, No. 403193
DOB: Dec. 26, 1912   **Place:** Torreon, Coahuila
Last Foreign Residence: Torreon, Coahuila
Married to: Maria Lopez   **Date:** June 27, 1940
Where: Topeka, Kansas (Maria was born in Horton, Kansas, on November 7, 1914.)   **Crossed the Border on:** April 26, 1915
Where: El Paso, Texas   **Mode of travel:** On foot (Certificate of Arrival, No. 16-R-9230)   **Date Certificate Issued:** June 27, 1940
Alien Registration: N.A.
Description: Occupation: Freezer. Two children listed – born in 1936 and 1939.

NATURALIZATION EXTRACTS

Name: David Aguilar
District Court: District Court, Southern District of California, Los Angeles, California **Address:** 4457½ Topaz St., Los Angeles, California
Type of Record: Declaration of Intention
DOB: Dec. 16, 1910 **Place:** Mexico City, Mexico
Last Foreign Residence: Mexico City, Mexico
Married to: Mary   **Date:** May 16, 1929
Where: Los Angeles, California (Mary was born at Mexico City, Mexico, in 1906. She entered the U.S. at El Paso, Texas, in 1924.) **Crossed the Border on:** December 31, 1925
Where: Calexico, California   **Mode of travel:** On foot (Certificate of Arrival, No. 23-133468) **Date Certificate Issued:** July 13, 1945
Alien Registration: N.A.
Description: Occupation: Dental Technician. Light Complexion, 5 Feet, 5 Inches, 150 Pounds, Brown Hair, Brown Eyes. Four children listed – all born between 1932 and 1940.

NATURALIZATION EXTRACTS

Name: Antonio Aguire
District Court: County Court, County of Maverick, Eagle Pass, Texas   **Address:** N.A.
Type of Record: Declaration of Intention
DOB: N.A. (23 years old)   **Place:** Monclova, Coahuila
Last Foreign Residence: N.A.
Married to: N.A.   **Date:** N.A.
Where: N.A.
Crossed the Border on: 1889
Where: Eagle Pass, Texas   **Mode of travel:** N.A.
Date Certificate Issued: October 21, 1896
Alien Registration: N.A.
Description: N.A.

NATURALIZATION EXTRACTS

Name: Tiburcio Aguire
District Court: County Court, County of Maverick, Eagle Pass, Texas   **Address:** N.A.
Type of Record: Declaration of Intention
DOB: N.A. (21 years old)   **Place:** Monclova, Coahuila
Last Foreign Residence: N.A.
Married to: N.A.   **Date:** N.A.
Where: N.A.
Crossed the Border on: 1885
Where: Eagle Pass, Texas   **Mode of travel:** N.A.
Date Certificate Issued: October 21, 1896
Alien Registration: N.A.
Description: N.A.

NATURALIZATION EXTRACTS

Name: Manuel Aguirre
District Court: County Court, County of Webb, Laredo, Texas **Address:** N.A.
Type of Record: Declaration of Intention, No. #1971
DOB: N.A. (26 years old) **Place:** Cadereyta, Nuevo Leon
Last Foreign Residence: N.A.
Married to: N.A.   **Date:** N.A.
Where: N.A.
Crossed the Border on: May 20, 1880
Where: Laredo, Texas   **Mode of travel:** N.A.
Date Certificate Issued: October 23, 1886
Alien Registration: N.A.
Description: N.A.

NATURALIZATION EXTRACTS

Name: Salvador Gonzales Aguirre
District Court: District Court, Los Angeles, California
Address: 533 Soldano Ave., Azusa, California
Type of Record: Petition for Naturalization, No. 71106 (No. 696287) **DOB:** June 29, 1909 **Place:** Encarnación, Jalisco
Last Foreign Residence: Zacatecas, Mexico
Married to: Josephine Abasta Aguirre **Date:** October 9, 1929 **Where:** Los Angeles, California (Josephine was born at El Paso, Texas, on August 27, 1913.) **Crossed the Border on:** June 29, 1915
Where: El Paso, Texas **Mode of travel:** Street Car (Certificate of Arrival, No. 23-R-63321) **Date Certificate Issued:** January 15, 1940
Alien Registration: N.A.
Description: Occupation: Laborer. Four children listed – born between 1930 and 1936.

NATURALIZATION EXTRACTS

Name: Jesus Alaners
District Court: County Court, County of Webb, Laredo, Texas **Address:** N.A.
Type of Record: Declaration of Intention
DOB: N.A. (42 years old) **Place:** Villa Santiago, Nuevo Leon **Last Foreign Residence:** N.A.
Married to: N.A.   **Date:** N.A.
Where: N.A.
Crossed the Border on: July 15, 1889
Where: Laredo, Texas **Mode of travel:** N.A.
Date Certificate Issued: November 5, 1892
Alien Registration: N.A.
Description: N.A.

NATURALIZATION EXTRACTS

Name: Celso Albias
District Court: County Court, County of Webb, Laredo, Texas **Address:** N.A.
Type of Record: Declaration of Intention
DOB: N.A. (36 years old) **Place:** Santa Gertrudes, Mexico
Last Foreign Residence: N.A.
Married to: N.A.   **Date:** N.A.
Where: N.A.
Crossed the Border on: July 2, 1870
Where: Los Tomates, Texas **Mode of travel:** N.A.
Date Certificate Issued: November 22, 1886
Alien Registration: N.A.
Description: N.A.

NATURALIZATION EXTRACTS

Name: Vicente Aldrete
District Court: County Court, County of Webb, Laredo, Texas
Address: N.A.
Type of Record: Declaration of Intention, No. #1910
DOB: N.A. (60 years old) **Place:** Santa Rosa, Mexico
Last Foreign Residence: N.A.
Married to: N.A.   **Date:** N.A.
Where: N.A.
Crossed the Border on: October 1847
Where: Eagle Pass, Texas **Mode of travel:** N.A.
Date Certificate Issued: October 29, 1886
Alien Registration: N.A.
Description: N.A.

NATURALIZATION EXTRACTS

Name: Andres Elvira Alemany
District Court: District Court, Southern District of California, Los Angeles, California **Address:** 1036 W. 20th St., Los Angeles, California
Type of Record: Declaration of Intention, No. 124502
DOB: July 12, 1895 **Place:** Huimanguillo, Tabasco
Last Foreign Residence: Tijuana, Baja California
Married to: Maria **Date:** May 14, 1928
Where: Laredo, Texas (Maria was born in Cozco, Peru, South America, on Dec. 25, 1900. She entered the U.S. at San Ysidro, California, on Sept. 11, 1942.) **Crossed the Border on:** May 1, 1943 (Crossed under the name of Andres E. Alemeny) **Where:** San Ysidro, California **Mode of travel:** On foot (Certificate of Arrival, No. 23-133421) **Date Certificate Issued:** July 12, 1945
Alien Registration: N.A.
Description: Occupation: Lawyer. Light Complexion, 5 Feet, 7 Inches, 225 Pounds, Gray Hair, Brown Eyes. Six children listed – all born between 1920 and 1932.

NATURALIZATION EXTRACTS

Name: Julio Almaraz
District Court: County Court, County of Webb, Laredo, Texas   **Address:** N.A.
Type of Record: Declaration of Intention, No. #2039
DOB: N.A. (68 years old) **Place:** Fresnillo, Zacatecas
Last Foreign Residence: N.A.
Married to: N.A. **Date:** N.A.
Where: N.A.
Crossed the Border on: 1875
Where: Laredo, Texas **Mode of travel:** N.A.
Date Certificate Issued: March 1, 1886
Alien Registration: N.A.
Description: N.A.

NATURALIZATION EXTRACTS

Name: Margarito Aranjo
District Court: District Court, District of Colorado, Denver, Colorado **Address:** 1989 S. Galapago St., Denver, Colorado
Type of Record: Declaration of Intention, No. 14110 (7477) **DOB:** Oct. 15, 1897   **Place:** Silao, Guanajuato
Last Foreign Residence: Silao, Guanajuato
Married to: Emeteria Aranjo   **Date:** Nov. 22, 1918
Where: Houston, Texas (Emeteria was born at Lagos de Moreno, Jalisco, on March 3, 1897. She entered the U.S. at Eagle Pass, Texas, date unknown.) **Crossed the Border on:** September 15, 1913
Where: Laredo, Texas   **Mode of travel:** Railroad (Certificate of Arrival, No. 19-14011) **Date Certificate Issued:** October 1, 1941 (A previous Declaration of Intention was filed in 1919 at the Denver District Court.) **Alien Registration:** N.A.
Description: Occupation: Moulder. Dark complexion, 5 Feet, 5 Inches, 135 Pounds, Black Hair, Brown Eyes. Seven children listed – all born between 1919 and 1932.

NATURALIZATION EXTRACTS

Name: Gabriel Archundia
District Court: District Court, Los Angeles, California
Address: 956 Hollins St., Los Angeles, California
Type of Record: Petition for Naturalization, No. 70817 (No. 695584) **DOB:** Nov. 18, 1897 **Place:** Mexico City, Mexico
Last Foreign Residence: Mexico City, Mexico
Married to: Maria M. Mendez **Date:** April 14, 1919
Where: Los Angeles, California (Maria was born at Parral, Chihuahua, on Nov. 21, 1898. She entered the U.S. at Los Angeles, California, on April 1, 1916.) **Crossed the Border on:** November 18, 1914
Where: El Paso, Texas **Mode of travel:** Street car (Certificate of Arrival, No. 23-36804) **Date Certificate Issued:** January 2, 1940 (Declaration of Intention 68299 (No. 14669) filed Dec. 24, 1934 in District Court, Los Angeles.) **Alien Registration:** N.A. **Description:** Occupation: Kitchen Helper. Dark Complexion. Dark Brown Eyes, Black Hair, 5 Feet, 4 Inches, 149 Pounds. Wife Maria was naturalized on July 27, 1935 in Los Angeles, California (Certificate No. 3983351).

NATURALIZATION EXTRACTS

Name: Joseph Arciga y Tovar (aka Joseph Arciga)
District Court: District Court, Southern District of California, Los Angeles, California **Address:** 2317 Juliet St., Los Angeles, California
Type of Record: Declaration of Intention
DOB: Nov. 2, 1914 **Place:** Mexico City, Mexico
Last Foreign Residence: Mexico City, Mexico
Married to: Helen   **Date:** Dec. 21, 1940
Where: Mexico City, Mexico (Helen was born at Chihuahua, Mexico, on Nov. 16, 1916. She entered the U.S. at El Paso, Texas, on Sept. 19, 1942.)
Crossed the Border on: September 19, 1942 (Crossed under the name of Jose Arciga y Tovar) **Where:** El Paso, Texas   **Mode of travel:** North Railroad of Mexico (Certificate of Arrival, No. 23-124377) **Date Certificate Issued:** August 3, 1945
Alien Registration: N.A.
Description: Occupation: Insurance Salesman. Dark Complexion, 5 Feet, 7 Inches, Brown Eyes, Black Hair, 165 Pounds. One child listed – born in 1942.

NATURALIZATION EXTRACTS

Name: Antonio Argola
District Court: County Court, County of Webb, Laredo, Texas **Address:** N.A.
Type of Record: Declaration of Intention, No. #1976
DOB: N.A. (51 years old) **Place:** Saltillo, Coahuila
Last Foreign Residence: N.A.
Married to: N.A.   **Date:** N.A.
Where: N.A.
Crossed the Border on: January 3, 1885
Where: Laredo, Texas **Mode of travel:** N.A.
Date Certificate Issued: October 23, 1886
Alien Registration: N.A.
Description: N.A.

NATURALIZATION EXTRACTS

Name: Irene Argumedo
District Court: District Court, District of Kansas
Address: 816 W. 11th St., Wichita, Kansas
Type of Record: Application to Take Oath of Allegiance
DOB: June 9, 1895   **Place:** Rago, Kansas
Last Foreign Residence: N.A.
Married to: Jose Argumedo   **Date:** August 9, 1934
Where: Wichita, Kansas (Jose was born in Sain Alto, Zacatecas.)   **Crossed the Border on:** N.A.
Where: N.A.   **Mode of travel:** N.A.
Date Certificate Issued: June 24, 1955
Alien Registration: N.A.
Description: Lost U.S. citizenship due to marriage on Oct. 22, 1913 to Joseana Mena, a subject of Mexico. Marriage Terminated July 13, 1928. Medium Complexion, Blue Eyes, Gray Hair, 5 Feet, 3 Inches, 190 Pounds.

NATURALIZATION EXTRACTS

Name: Rafael Ariola
District Court: County Court, County of Webb, Laredo, Texas **Address:** N.A.
Type of Record: Declaration of Intention
DOB: N.A. (22 years old) **Place:** Montemorelos, Nuevo Leon **Last Foreign Residence:** N.A.
Married to: N.A.   **Date:** N.A.
Where: N.A.
Crossed the Border on: July 6, 1888
Where: Laredo, Texas   **Mode of travel:** N.A.
Date Certificate Issued: October 31, 1890
Alien Registration: N.A.
Description: N.A.

NATURALIZATION EXTRACTS

Name: Anastacio Arisola
District Court: County Court, County of Webb, Laredo, Texas **Address:** N.A.
Type of Record: Declaration of Intention
DOB: N.A. (33 years old) **Place:** Nuevo Laredo, Tamaulipas **Last Foreign Residence:** N.A.
Married to: N.A.   **Date:** N.A.
Where: N.A.
Crossed the Border on: July 17, 1883
Where: Laredo, Texas **Mode of travel:** N.A.
Date Certificate Issued: November 1, 1890
Alien Registration: N.A.
Description: N.A.

NATURALIZATION EXTRACTS

Name: Panciano Arisola
District Court: County Court, County of Webb, Laredo, Texas **Address:** N.A.
Type of Record: Declaration of Intention
DOB: N.A. (22 years old)   **Place:** Nuevo Laredo, Tamaulipas **Last Foreign Residence:** N.A.
Married to: N.A.   **Date:** N.A.
Where: N.A.
Crossed the Border on: June 1, 1887
Where: Laredo, Texas   **Mode of travel:** N.A.
Date Certificate Issued: November 1, 1890
Alien Registration: N.A.
Description: N.A.

NATURALIZATION EXTRACTS

Name: Felix Armendariz
District Court: Superior Court, Cochise County, State of Arizona   **Address:** 626 4th St., Douglas, Arizona
Type of Record: Declaration of Intention, No. 843 (107350)   **DOB:** April 10, 1894   **Place:** Ocampo, Chihuahua
Last Foreign Residence: Ocampo, Chihuahua
Married to: N.A.   **Date:** N.A.
Where: N.A.
Crossed the Border on: August 4, 1903
Where: Douglas, Arizona   **Mode of travel:** Walked across   **Date Certificate Issued:** May 9, 1916
Alien Registration: N.A.
Description: Occupation: Hotel Clerk. Dark Complexion, 5 Feet, 4 Inches, 129 Pounds, Black Hair, Brown Eyes.

NATURALIZATION EXTRACTS

Name: Mauro Armendariz

District Court: District Court, Los Angeles, California

Address: 1668 15th St., Santa Monica, California

Type of Record: Petition for Naturalization, No. 70878 (No. 695875)
DOB: July 16, 1899 **Place:** Parral, Chihuahua

Last Foreign Residence: Parral, Chihuahua

Married to: Elena A.   **Date:** July 9, 1919

Where: El Paso, Texas (Elena was born at Santa Rosalia, Mexico, on Aug. 18, 1897. She entered the U.S. at El Paso, Texas, on Nov. 8, 1918.)
Crossed the Border on: February 2, 1921

Where: El Paso, Texas **Mode of travel:** El Paso Electric Railway (Certificate of Arrival, No. 23-48374)
Date Certificate Issued: January 4, 1940 (Declaration of Intention 81179 filed May 15, 1937 in Circuit Court, Los Angeles.)
Alien Registration: N.A.

Description: Occupation: Laborer. Seven children listed – all born between 1920 and 1933.

NATURALIZATION EXTRACTS

Name: Martin Arrevalos
District Court: County Court, County of Webb, Laredo, Texas **Address:** N.A.
Type of Record: Declaration of Intention
DOB: N.A. (43 years old) **Place:** Matehuala, San Luis Potosi **Last Foreign Residence:** N.A.
Married to: N.A. **Date:** N.A.
Where: N.A.
Crossed the Border on: April 22, 1885
Where: Laredo, Texas **Mode of travel:** N.A.
Date Certificate Issued: November 7, 1892
Alien Registration: N.A.
Description: N.A.

NATURALIZATION EXTRACTS

Name: Guillermo Arriola
District Court: District Court, Los Angeles, California
Address: 2015 E. 45th St., Los Angeles, California
Type of Record: Petition for Naturalization, No. 71095 (696184)   **DOB:** Dec. 21, 1906   **Place:** Hermosillo, Sonora
Last Foreign Residence: Tijuana, Baja California
Married to: Concha Arias   **Date:** April 6, 1939
Where: Los Angeles, California (Concha was born at Compton, California, on April 16, 1916.)   **Crossed the Border on:** August 30, 1916
Where: Nogales, Arizona **Mode of travel:** Foot (Certificate of Arrival, No. 23-56691)   **Date Certificate Issued:** January 15, 1940
Alien Registration: N.A.
Description: Occupation: Candy Maker. Two children listed – born in 1938 and 1939.

NATURALIZATION EXTRACTS

Name: Pablo Barrejo
District Court: County Court, County of Webb, Laredo, Texas **Address:** N.A.
Type of Record: Declaration of Intention, No. 1895
DOB: N.A. (70 years old) **Place:** Bustamante, Nuevo Leon **Last Foreign Residence:** N.A.
Married to: N.A.　　　**Date:** N.A.
Where: N.A.
Crossed the Border on: July 3, 1882
Where: Laredo, Texas **Mode of travel:** N.A.
Date Certificate Issued: October 30, 1886
Alien Registration: N.A.
Description: N.A.

NATURALIZATION EXTRACTS

Name: Chris Bartch
District Court: Superior Court, Cochise County, State of Arizona **Address:** Box 681, Bisbee, Arizona
Type of Record: Declaration of Intention, No. 939 (328641) **DOB:** March 14, 1895   **Place:** Chihuahua, Mexico
Last Foreign Residence: Chihuahua, Mexico
Married to: N.A.   **Date:** N.A.
Where: N.A.
Crossed the Border on: September 1, 1901
Where: El Paso, Texas   **Mode of travel:** Mexican Central Railroad **Date Certificate Issued:** December 8, 1916
Alien Registration: N.A.
Description: Occupation: Clerk. Fair Complexion, 5 Feet, 8 Inches, 146 Pounds, Red Hair, Blue Eyes.

NATURALIZATION EXTRACTS

Name: Estela Belendez
District Court: District Court, Los Angeles, California
Address: 1111 W. 46th St., Los Angeles, California
Type of Record: Petition for Naturalization, No. 70844 (695882) **DOB:** April 28, 1910 **Place:** Arizpe, Sonora
Last Foreign Residence: Nacozari, Sonora
Married to: Ignacio Belendez **Date:** October 8, 1933
Where: Los Angeles, California (Ignacio was born in Agua Prieta, Sonora, on Feb. 7, 1909. He entered the U.S. at Douglas, Arizona, on Oct. 25, 1920.) **Crossed the Border on:** April 19, 1915
Where: Douglas, Arizona **Mode of travel:** Foot (Certificate of Arrival, No. 23-41218)
Date Certificate Issued: January 2, 1940 (Declaration of Intention 77706 filed on Sept. 10, 1936 in District Court, Los Angeles, California) **Alien Registration:** N.A.
Description: Occupation: Head cashier. Fair Complexion, Brown Eyes, Dark Brown Hair, 5 Feet, 1 Inch, 108 Pounds. Resided in Los Angeles County since 1923.

NATURALIZATION EXTRACTS

Name: Ignacio Belendez aka Francisco Ignacio Belendez
District Court: District Court, Los Angeles, California
Address: 1111 W. 46th St., Los Angeles, California (534 ½ W. 53rd St., Los Angeles, in the Declaration of Intention) **Type of Record:** Petition for Naturalization, No. 70843 (695883)
DOB: Feb. 7, 1909   **Place:** Agua Prieta, Sonora
Last Foreign Residence: Agua Prieta, Sonora
Married to: Estelle   **Date:** October 8, 1933
Where: Los Angeles, California (Estelle was born in Arizpe, Sonora, on April 28, 1910. She entered the U.S. at Douglas, Arizona, on April 19, 1915.)
Crossed the Border on: October 25, 1920 (Crossed under the name of Ignacio Belendez) **Where:** Douglas, Arizona   **Mode of travel:** On foot
Date Certificate Issued: January 2, 1940 (Declaration of Intention 74390 filed on Feb. 18, 1936 in District Court, Los Angeles, California) **Alien Registration:** N.A.
Description: Occupation: Salesman. Resided in Los Angeles County since 1921.

NATURALIZATION EXTRACTS

Name: Guadalupe Bergandi
District Court: District Court, Los Angeles, California
Address: 1102 N. Alma Ave., Los Angeles, California
Type of Record: Petition for Naturalization, No. 71177 (696036)
DOB: Dec. 30, 1893　　**Place:** Rosario, Sinaloa
Last Foreign Residence: Mexico City, Mexico
Married to: Frank Bergandi　**Date:** Feb. 20, 1926
Where: Los Angeles, California (Frank was born at Mazzo, Italy, on June 9, 1890. She entered the U.S. at New York, New York, on 1922.)
Crossed the Border on: December 22, 1922 (Crossed under the name of Guadalupe Moreno)
Where: El Paso, Texas　**Mode of travel:** National Railway of Mexico (Certificate of Arrival, No. 23-72478)
Date Certificate Issued: January 18, 1940
Alien Registration: N.A.
Description: Occupation: Housekeeping. One child listed – born in 1929. Husband Frank Bergandi was naturalized on April 6, 1928, at District Court in Los Angeles, California.

NATURALIZATION EXTRACTS

Name: Mauro Borjas
District Court: District Court, Ft. Scott, Kansas
Address: 1011 N. Lincoln, Chanute, Kansas
Type of Record: Declaration of Intention
DOB: Nov. 22, 1901 **Place:** Irapuato, Guanajuato
Last Foreign Residence: Irapuato, Guanajuato
Married to: Tiodora Gutierrez Borjas **Date:** Oct. 26, 1918 **Where:** Chanute, Kansas (Tiodora was born at La Puerta de St. Juan, Guanajuato, on Nov. 4, 1904. She entered the U.S. at Laredo, Texas, in 1915.)
Crossed the Border on: October 15, 1920
Where: Laredo, Texas **Mode of travel:** Footbridge (Certificate of Arrival, No. 16-12513)
Date Certificate Issued: December 24, 1941 (Departed the U.S. at Laredo on August 1924, Returned to the U.S. at Laredo in January 1925)
Alien Registration: N.A.
Description: Occupation: Cement Plant Laborer. Dark Complexion, Brown Eyes, Black Hair, 5 Feet, 5½ Inches, 175 Pounds. Three children listed – all born between 1919 and 1926.

NATURALIZATION EXTRACTS

Name: Antonio Estrada Bray
District Court: Superior Court, Cochise County, State of Arizona **Address:** 317 9th Street, Douglas, Arizona
Type of Record: Declaration of Intention, No. 786 (97628)
DOB: May 20, 1893   **Place:** Cunepas, Sonora
Last Foreign Residence: Nacozari, Sonora
Married to: N.A.   **Date:** N.A.
Where: N.A.
Crossed the Border on: May 1, 1913
Where: Douglas, Arizona   **Mode of travel:** Nacozari Railroad **Date Certificate Issued:** August 19, 1915
Alien Registration: N.A.
Description: Occupation: Mechanic. Dark Complexion, 5 Feet, 7 Inches, 146 Pounds, Black Hair, Brown Eyes.

NATURALIZATION EXTRACTS

Name: Bruno Bueno
District Court: County Court, County of Webb, Laredo, Texas   **Address:** N.A.
Type of Record: Declaration of Intention
DOB: N.A. (44 years old) **Place:** Saltillo, Coahuila
Last Foreign Residence: N.A.
Married to: N.A.   **Date:** N.A.
Where: N.A.
Crossed the Border on: April 1, 1886
Where: Laredo, Texas **Mode of travel:** N.A.
Date Certificate Issued: October 31, 1890
Alien Registration: N.A.
Description: N.A.

NATURALIZATION EXTRACTS

Name: Jose Antonio Calero
District Court: District Court, Southern District of California, Los Angeles, California   **Address:** 758 East 76th Place, Los Angeles, California
Type of Record: Declaration of Intention, No. 124607
DOB: Aug. 3, 1914 **Place:** Gomez Palacios, Durango
Last Foreign Residence: Gomez Palacios, Durango
Married to: Maria   **Date:** January 15, 1944
Where: Torreon, Coahuila (Maria was born in Parral, Chihuahua, on July 16, 1925. She entered the U.S. at El Paso, Texas in June 1945.)   **Crossed the Border on:** May 2, 1945 (Crossed under the name of Jose Calero Garza)   **Where:** El Paso, Texas   **Mode of travel:** North Railroad of Mexico (Certificate of Arrival, No. 23-133643)   **Date Certificate Issued:** August 11, 1945
Alien Registration: N.A.
Description: Occupation: Auto Mechanic. Medium Complexion, Hazel Eyes, Brown Hair, 5 Feet, 9 Inches, 160 Pounds. Two children listed – all born between 1944 and 1945.

NATURALIZATION EXTRACTS

Name: Marcelino Cano
District Court: County Court, County of Maverick, Eagle Pass, Texas   **Address:** N.A.
Type of Record: Declaration of Intention
DOB: N.A. (21 years old) **Place:** Parras, Coahuila
Last Foreign Residence: N.A.
Married to: N.A. **Date:** N.A.
Where: N.A.
Crossed the Border on: July 5, 1891
Where: Eagle Pass, Texas **Mode of travel:** N.A.
Date Certificate Issued: October 26, 1896
Alien Registration: N.A.
Description: N.A.

NATURALIZATION EXTRACTS

Name: Felipe Cardenaz
District Court: Superior Court, Cochise County, State of Arizona   **Address:** 351 10th Street, Douglas, Arizona
Type of Record: Declaration of Intention, No. 1018 (293375)   **DOB:** May 1, 1891   **Place:** Chihuahua, Chihuahua
Last Foreign Residence: Chihuahua, Chihuahua
Married to: Matilda Morales de Cardenaz   **Date:** N.A.   **Where:** N.A. (Matilda was born at Rayon, Sonora.)
Crossed the Border on: June 1907
Where: El Paso, Texas   **Mode of travel:** El Paso Street Railway   **Date Certificate Issued:** June 13, 1917
Alien Registration: N.A.
Description: Occupation: Kitchen Work. Dark Complexion, 5 Feet, 5 Inches, 130 Pounds, Black Hair, Brown Eyes.

NATURALIZATION EXTRACTS

Name: Cruz Carlin (formerly Maria Cruz Gutierrez)
District Court: District Court, District of Colorado, Denver, Colorado **Address:** 4324 Delaware Street, Denver, Colorado
Type of Record: Declaration of Intention, No. 14497 (20780) **DOB:** Sept. 5, 1909 **Place:** Guadalupe, Jalisco
Last Foreign Residence: Juarez, Chihuahua
Married to: Frank Carlin **Date:** August 20, 1927
Where: Juarez, Chihuahua (Frank was born on March 31, 1904 at Valle Guadalupe, Mexico. He entered the U.S. at El Paso, Texas, on August 22, 1927.)
Crossed the Border on: August 23, 1927 (Crossed under the name of Maria Cruz Gutierrez)
Where: El Paso, Texas **Mode of travel:** El Paso Electric Railway (Certificate of Arrival, No. 18-13598)
Date Certificate Issued: August 6, 1943
Alien Registration: N.A.
Description: Occupation: Housewife. Dark complexion, 5 Feet, 2 Inches, 135 Pounds, Black Hair, Green Eyes. Three children listed – all born between 1928 and 1933.

NATURALIZATION EXTRACTS

Name: Soledad Carrasco
District Court: District Court, District of Colorado, Denver, Colorado **Address:** 2123 Lawrence St., Denver, Colorado
Type of Record: Declaration of Intention, No. 14562 (21080) **DOB:** Sept. 25, 1906   **Place:** Camargo, Chihuahua
Last Foreign Residence: Camargo, Chihuahua
Married to: Not married   **Date:** N.A.
Where: N.A.
Crossed the Border on: Jan. 13, 1919
Where: El Paso, Texas   **Mode of travel:** El Paso Electric Railway (Certificate of Arrival, No. 18-14000) **Date Certificate Issued:** April 1, 1944
Alien Registration: N.A.
Description: Occupation: Machine Operator. Dark complexion, 5 Feet, ¾ Inches, 145 Pounds, Brown Hair, Brown Eyes.

NATURALIZATION EXTRACTS

Name: Louis M. Carrilla
District Court: Superior Court, Cochise County, State of Arizona   **Address:** Box 61, Pirtherville, Arizona
Type of Record: Declaration of Intention, No. 968 (328671)   **DOB:** August 24, 1875 **Place:** Arizpe, Sonora
Last Foreign Residence: Sahuaripa, Sonora
Married to: N.A. **Date:** N.A.
Where: N.A.
Crossed the Border on: March 1911
Where: Douglas, Arizona **Mode of travel:** Nacozari Railroad   **Date Certificate Issued:** March 16, 1917
Alien Registration: N.A.
Description: Occupation: Storekeeper. Dark Complexion, 5 Feet, 8 Inches, 120 Pounds, Black Hair, Black Eyes.

NATURALIZATION EXTRACTS

Name: Abran P. Casanova

District Court: County Court, County of Webb, Laredo, Texas
Address: N.A.

Type of Record: Declaration of Intention

DOB: N.A. (34 years old)　　**Place:** Matamoros, Tamaulipas
Last Foreign Residence: N.A.

Married to: N.A.　　　　**Date:** N.A.

Where: N.A.

Crossed the Border on: June 1882

Where: Brownsville, Texas　**Mode of travel:** N.A.

Date Certificate Issued: January 31, 1906

Alien Registration: N.A.

Description: N.A.

NATURALIZATION EXTRACTS

Name: Alfonso Castillo
District Court: Superior Court, Cochise County, State of Arizona **Address:** 312 E. Avenue, Douglas, Arizona
Type of Record: Declaration of Intention, No. 965 (328668) **DOB:** Jan. 23, 1879   **Place:** Chihuahua, Mexico
Last Foreign Residence: Juarez, Chihuahua
Married to: Not married   **Date:** N.A.
Where: N.A.
Crossed the Border on: April 5, 1895
Where: El Paso, Texas   **Mode of travel:** Walked across **Date Certificate Issued:** March 7, 1917
Alien Registration: N.A.
Description: Occupation: Mechanic Helper. Dark Complexion, 5 Feet, 6 Inches, 140 Pounds, Black Hair, Brown Eyes.

NATURALIZATION EXTRACTS

Name: Guadalupe Cano Castillo
District Court: District Court, Southern District of California, Los Angeles, California **Address:** 443 N. Ezra St., Los Angeles, California
Type of Record: Declaration of Intention, No. 125814
DOB: Dec. 9, 1903 **Place:** Valle de Allende, Chihuahua
Last Foreign Residence: Chihuahua, Mexico
Married to: Eulalio **Date:** Sept. 28, 1924
Where: Los Angeles, California (Eulalio was born in Santa Maria de Los Angeles, Mexico, on Feb. 13, 1889. He entered the U.S. at El Paso, Texas, on July 15, 1906.)
Crossed the Border on: August 12, 1914 (Crossed under the name of Guadalupe Cano)
Where: El Paso, Texas **Mode of travel:** Foot (Certificate of Arrival, No. 23-134724)
Date Certificate Issued: May 1, 1946
Alien Registration: N.A.
Description: Occupation: Housewife. Medium Complexion, 5 Feet, 1 Inch, Brown Eyes, Black/Grey Hair, 150 Pounds. Two children listed – born in 1924 and 1926.

NATURALIZATION EXTRACTS

Name: Esteban Castro
District Court: County Court, County of Webb, Laredo, Texas **Address:** N.A.
Type of Record: Declaration of Intention
DOB: N.A. (26 years old) **Place:** Monterrey, Nuevo Leon
Last Foreign Residence: N.A.
Married to: N.A.   **Date:** N.A.
Where: N.A.
Crossed the Border on: October 8, 1888
Where: Laredo, Texas **Mode of travel:** N.A.
Date Certificate Issued: October 31, 1888
Alien Registration: N.A.
Description: N.A.

NATURALIZATION EXTRACTS

Name: Isiderio Castro
District Court: County Court, County of Maverick, Eagle Pass, Texas   **Address:** N.A.
Type of Record: Declaration of Intention
DOB: N.A. (22 years old)   **Place:** Monclova, Coahuila
Last Foreign Residence: N.A.
Married to: N.A.   **Date:** N.A.
Where: N.A.
Crossed the Border on: October 1874
Where: Eagle Pass, Texas   **Mode of travel:** N.A.
Date Certificate Issued: October 31, 1884
Alien Registration: N.A.
Description: N.A.

NATURALIZATION EXTRACTS

Name: Milton Castro
District Court: Superior Court, Cochise County, State of Arizona **Address:** Bisbee, Arizona
Type of Record: Declaration of Intention, No. 712 (97557)
DOB: April 1, 1881 **Place:** Sacualco, Ays Canton, Mexico
Last Foreign Residence: Guadalajara, Jalisco
Married to: N.A. **Date:** N.A.
Where: N.A.
Crossed the Border on: May 20, 1904
Where: El Paso, Texas **Mode of travel:** Central Railroad **Date Certificate Issued:** Dec. 9, 1914
Alien Registration: N.A.
Description: Occupation: Laborer. Dark Complexion, 5 Feet, 6 Inches, 135 Pounds, Black Hair, Gray Eyes.

NATURALIZATION EXTRACTS

Name: Ignacio Chapa
District Court: County Court, County of Webb, Laredo, Texas   **Address:** N.A.
Type of Record: Declaration of Intention
DOB: N.A. (25 years old) **Place:** Sabinas Hidalgo, Nuevo Leon   **Last Foreign Residence:** N.A.
Married to: N.A.   **Date:** N.A.
Where: N.A.
Crossed the Border on: April 15, 1887
Where: Laredo, Texas **Mode of travel:** N.A.
Date Certificate Issued: November 7, 1892
Alien Registration: N.A.
Description: N.A.

NATURALIZATION EXTRACTS

Name: Juan C. Chapa
District Court: County Court, County of Webb, Laredo, Texas
Address: N.A.
Type of Record: Declaration of Intention
DOB: N.A. (21 years old) **Place:** Cerralvo, Nuevo Leon
Last Foreign Residence: N.A.
Married to: N.A.   **Date:** N.A.
Where: N.A.
Crossed the Border on: N.A.
Where: Carrizo, Texas **Mode of travel:** N.A.
Date Certificate Issued: November 7, 1892
Alien Registration: N.A.
Description: N.A.

NATURALIZATION EXTRACTS

Name: Bernardino Chavez

District Court: County Court, County of Webb, Laredo, Texas
Address: N.A.

Type of Record: Declaration of Intention

DOB: N.A. (44 years old) **Place:** Cadereyta, Nuevo Leon

Last Foreign Residence: N.A.

Married to: N.A.   **Date:** N.A.

Where: N.A.

Crossed the Border on: May 20, 1858

Where: Carrizo, Texas **Mode of travel:** N.A.

Date Certificate Issued: November 7, 1892

Alien Registration: N.A.

Description: N.A.

NATURALIZATION EXTRACTS

Name: Pablo Chavez
District Court: District Court, District of Colorado, Denver, Colorado   **Address:** 514 West 6th St., Pueblo, Colorado
Type of Record: Declaration of Intention, No. 14644 (21364)   **DOB:** June 29, 1910   **Place:** Laredo, Durango
Last Foreign Residence: Laredo, Durango
Married to: Not married   **Date:** N.A.
Where: N.A.
Crossed the Border on: Dec. 11, 1914
Where: El Paso, Texas   **Mode of travel:** Train (Certificate of Arrival, No. 19-R-16971)   **Date Certificate Issued:** Sept. 17, 1945
Alien Registration: N.A.
Description: Occupation: Section Laborer. Dark complexion, 5 Feet, 3 Inches, 136 Pounds, Black Hair, Brown Eyes.

NATURALIZATION EXTRACTS

Name: Elijio Cisneros
District Court: County Court, County of Webb, Laredo, Texas
Address: N.A.
Type of Record: Declaration of Intention
DOB: N.A. (72 years old) **Place:** Acapulco, Mexico
Last Foreign Residence: N.A.
Married to: N.A.   **Date:** N.A.
Where: N.A.
Crossed the Border on: March 2, 1863
Where: Laredo, Texas   **Mode of travel:** N.A.
Date Certificate Issued: January 26, 1906
Alien Registration: N.A.
Description: N.A.

NATURALIZATION EXTRACTS

Name: Lucio Contreras
District Court: County Court, County of Webb, Laredo, Texas **Address:** N.A.
Type of Record: Declaration of Intention, No. #1931
DOB: N.A. (25 years old) **Place:** Monterrey, Nuevo Leon
Last Foreign Residence: N.A.
Married to: N.A.   **Date:** N.A.
Where: N.A.
Crossed the Border on: April 10, 1883
Where: Laredo, Texas **Mode of travel:** N.A.
Date Certificate Issued: October 27, 1886
Alien Registration: N.A.
Description: N.A.

NATURALIZATION EXTRACTS

Name: Alvino Cortina
District Court: County Court, County of Webb, Laredo, Texas **Address:** N.A.
Type of Record: Declaration of Intention
DOB: N.A. (40 years old) **Place:** Villa de Mina, Mexico
Last Foreign Residence: N.A.
Married to: N.A.   **Date:** N.A.
Where: N.A.
Crossed the Border on: February 5, 1891
Where: Laredo, Texas **Mode of travel:** N.A.
Date Certificate Issued: November 7, 1892
Alien Registration: N.A.
Description: N.A.

NATURALIZATION EXTRACTS

Name: Salomon S. Coy
District Court: County Court, County of Maverick, Eagle Pass, Texas **Address:** N.A.
Type of Record: Declaration of Intention
DOB: N.A. (49 years old) **Place:** Cuatro Cienegas, Coahuila **Last Foreign Residence:** N.A.
Married to: N.A.   **Date:** N.A.
Where: N.A.
Crossed the Border on: 1864
Where: Eagle Pass, Texas **Mode of travel:** N.A.
Date Certificate Issued: October 25, 1894
Alien Registration: N.A.
Description: N.A.

NATURALIZATION EXTRACTS

Name: Juan Cruz
District Court: County Court, County of Webb, Laredo, Texas **Address:** N.A.
Type of Record: Declaration of Intention
DOB: N.A. (29 years old) **Place:** Sabinas Hidalgo, Nuevo Leon **Last Foreign Residence:** N.A.
Married to: N.A.   **Date:** N.A.
Where: N.A.
Crossed the Border on: June 1903
Where: Laredo, Texas   **Mode of travel:** N.A.
Date Certificate Issued: June 9, 1906
Alien Registration: N.A.
Description: N.A.

NATURALIZATION EXTRACTS

Name: Simitrio Correa Davila
District Court: District Court, Southern District of California, Los Angeles, California **Address:** 103 N. Boyle Ave., Los Angeles, California
Type of Record: Declaration of Intention
DOB: May 6, 1906 **Place:** Mexico City, Mexico
Last Foreign Residence: Mexico City, Mexico
Married to: Estela **Date:** Feb. 9, 1939
Where: Mexico City, Mexico (Estela was born at Taxco, Mexico, on Dec. 22, 1908. She entered the U.S. at El Paso, Texas, on Dec. 12, 1944.) **Crossed the Border on:** December 12, 1944 (Crossed under the name of Simitrio Davila Correa) **Where:** El Paso, Texas **Mode of travel:** National Railroad of Mexico (Certificate of Arrival, No. 23-132523) **Date Certificate Issued:** August 10, 1945
Alien Registration: N.A.
Description: Occupation: Head Waiter. Dark Complexion, 6 Feet, 0 Inches, Brown Eyes, Black Hair, 148 Pounds. One child listed – born in 1927.

NATURALIZATION EXTRACTS

Name: Martin de la Rosa
District Court: County Court, County of Webb, Laredo, Texas **Address:** N.A.
Type of Record: Declaration of Intention
DOB: N.A. (28 years old) **Place:** Real de Catorce, San Luis Potosi **Last Foreign Residence:** N.A.
Married to: N.A.   **Date:** N.A.
Where: N.A.
Crossed the Border on: June 15, 1887
Where: Laredo, Texas **Mode of travel:** N.A.
Date Certificate Issued: November 7, 1892
Alien Registration: N.A.
Description: N.A.

NATURALIZATION EXTRACTS

Name: Tomas de la Rosa
District Court: County Court, County of Webb, Laredo, Texas **Address:** N.A.
Type of Record: Declaration of Intention
DOB: N.A. (29 years old) **Place:** Zacatecas, Mexico
Last Foreign Residence: N.A.
Married to: N.A.   **Date:** N.A.
Where: N.A.
Crossed the Border on: January 22, 1902
Where: Laredo, Texas **Mode of travel:** N.A.
Date Certificate Issued: January 29, 1906
Alien Registration: N.A.
Description: N.A.

NATURALIZATION EXTRACTS

Name: Esmerjildo Delgado
District Court: County Court, County of Maverick, Eagle Pass, Texas **Address:** N.A.
Type of Record: Declaration of Intention
DOB: N.A. (25 years old) **Place:** Nuevo Laredo, Tamaulipas **Last Foreign Residence:** N.A.
Married to: N.A. **Date:** N.A.
Where: N.A.
Crossed the Border on: October 22, 1884
Where: Eagle Pass, Texas **Mode of travel:** N.A.
Date Certificate Issued: October 19, 1886
Alien Registration: N.A.
Description: N.A.

NATURALIZATION EXTRACTS

Name: Julia Estrada Delgado
District Court: District Court, Southern District of California, Los Angeles, California **Address:** 157½ N. Alma Ave., Los Angeles, California
Type of Record: Declaration of Intention, No. 125787
DOB: Feb. 16, 1901 **Place:** Todos Santos, Baja California
Last Foreign Residence: La Paz, Baja California
Married to: Jose (widowed) **Date:** Oct. 6, 1923
Where: Santa Ana, California (Jose was born in La Piedad, Michoacan, on May 3, 1901. He entered the U.S. at Nogales, Arizona. Now deceased.)
Crossed the Border on: August 28, 1922 (Crossed under the name of Julia Estrada)
Where: Nogales, Arizona **Mode of travel:** Foot (Certificate of Arrival, No. 1600-K-1952)
Date Certificate Issued: April 26, 1946
Alien Registration: N.A.
Description: Occupation: Seamstress. Medium Complexion, 5 Feet, ½ Inch, 124 Pounds, Black/Grey Hair, Brown Eyes.

NATURALIZATION EXTRACTS

Name: Valente Delgado aka Valentine Delgadillo

District Court: District Court, District of Colorado, Denver, Colorado **Address:** 1835 Platte Street, Denver, Colorado

Type of Record: Declaration of Intention, No. 147156 (21589) **DOB:** May 21, 1901　**Place:** Mesticca [Mexticacan], Jalisco **Last Foreign Residence:** Mesticcan [Mexticacan], Jalisco

Married to: Guadalupe Delgado　**Date:** April 15, 1925

Where: Pueblo, Colorado (Guadalupe was born at Mexico City, Mexico, on Dec. 19, 1905. She entered the U.S. at El Paso, Texas, on February 13, 1917.) **Crossed the Border on:** January 21, 1918 (Crossed under the name of Valentine Delgadillo) **Where:** El Paso, Texas　**Mode of travel:** On foot (Certificate of Arrival, No. 18 R 10996) **Date Certificate Issued:** March 13, 1947

Alien Registration: N.A.

Description: Occupation: Laborer. Dark complexion, 5 Feet, 3 Inches, 133 Pounds, Black Hair, Brown Eyes. Six children listed – all born between 1926 and 1935.

NATURALIZATION EXTRACTS

Name: Cruz Vasquez Chavez Diaz
District Court: District Court, Southern District of California, Los Angeles, California **Address:** 437 S. Del Mar, San Gabriel, California
Type of Record: Declaration of Intention, No. 125740
DOB: March 17, 1911 **Place:** Batopilas, Chihuahua
Last Foreign Residence: Batopilas, Chihuahua
Married to: Anthony Diaz **Date:** Jan. 10, 1946
Where: Las Vegas, Nevada (Anthony was born in Aguascalientes, Mexico, on Dec. 23, 1920. He entered the U.S. at Nogales, Arizona, on Jan. 5, 1946.) **Crossed the Border on:** February 15, 1916 (Crossed under the name of Cruz Vasquez Lastre) **Where:** El Paso, Texas **Mode of travel:** On foot (Certificate of Arrival, No. 23-127481) **Date Certificate Issued:** April 19, 1945
Alien Registration: N.A.
Description: Occupation: Cafe Operator. Olive Complexion, 5 Feet, 2 Inches, 135 Pounds, Black Hair, Brown Eyes. Three children – all born between 1929 and 1934.

NATURALIZATION EXTRACTS

Name: Guadalupe Navarro Diaz
District Court: District Court, Southern District of California, Los Angeles, California **Address:** 2018 Rome Dr., Los Angeles, California
Type of Record: Declaration of Intention
DOB: Dec. 12, 1897 **Place:** Arandas, Jalisco
Last Foreign Residence: Aguascalientes, Mexico
Married to: Angelina   **Date:** September 3, 1921
Where: Los Angeles, California (Angelina was born at La Union, Chihuahua, on May 30, 1898. She entered the U.S. at Naco, Arizona, on April 15, 1920.) **Crossed the Border on:** February 18, 1905
Where: El Paso, Texas   **Mode of travel:** On foot
Date Certificate Issued: July 24, 1945
Alien Registration: N.A.
Description: Occupation: Painter. Light Brown Complexion, Brown Eyes, Brown Hair, 5 Feet, 7 Inches, 165 Pounds. Five children – all born between 1924 and 1930.

NATURALIZATION EXTRACTS

Name: Martin Diaz
District Court: District Court, Los Angeles, California
Address: 349 South Ave., Los Angeles, California
Type of Record: Petition for Naturalization, No. 695729
DOB: Nov. 11, 1897 **Place:** Aguascalientes, Mexico
Last Foreign Residence: Aguascalientes, Mexico
Married to: Refugio   **Date:** October 12, 1924
Where: Los Angeles, California (Refugio was born in Cieneguilla, Aguascalientes, on Aug. 18, 1894. She entered the U.S. at El Paso, Texas, in Sept. 1920.)   **Crossed the Border on:** July 3, 1920
Where: Laredo, Texas **Mode of travel:** Footbridge (Certificate of Arrival, No. 23-29713)   **Date Certificate Issued:** January 5, 1940 (Declaration of Intention 64353 (No. 99021) filed on Jan. 20, 1934 in District Court, Los Angeles, California)   **Alien Registration:** N.A.
Description: Occupation: Laborer. Dark Complexion, Brown Eyes, Black Hair, 5 Feet, 8 Inches, 174 Pounds. Four children listed – all born between 1920 and 1934.

NATURALIZATION EXTRACTS

Name: Santos Dominguez
District Court: County Court, County of Maverick, Eagle Pass, Texas **Address:** N.A.
Type of Record: Declaration of Intention
DOB: N.A. (45 years old)   **Place:** Presidio del Norte [now Ojinaga], Chihuahua **Last Foreign Residence:** N.A.
Married to: N.A.   **Date:** N.A.
Where: N.A.
Crossed the Border on: June 25, 1866
Where: Eagle Pass, Texas   **Mode of travel:** N.A.
Date Certificate Issued: October 16, 1886
Alien Registration: N.A.
Description: N.A.

NATURALIZATION EXTRACTS

Name: Horacio Enriquez
District Court: District Court, Los Angeles, California
Address: 451½ E. 48th St., Los Angeles, California
Type of Record: Petition for Naturalization, No. 71052 (695824)   **DOB:** Jan. 3, 1913   **Place:** Chihuahua, Chihuahua
Last Foreign Residence: Juarez, Chihuahua
Married to: Margarita Reyes   **Date:** Dec. 7, 1936
Where: El Paso, Texas (Margarita was born in El Paso, Texas, on June 7, 1919.)   **Crossed the Border on:** April 28, 1921
Where: El Paso, Texas   **Mode of travel:** Street car (Certificate of Arrival, No. 25-4407)   **Date Certificate Issued:** January 11, 1940
Alien Registration: N.A.
Description: Occupation: Mailer, L.A. Examiner. Two children listed – born in 1937 and 1939.

NATURALIZATION EXTRACTS

Name: Amado Esparza
District Court: County Court, County of Webb, Laredo, Texas
Address: N.A.
Type of Record: Declaration of Intention
DOB: N.A. (45 years old) **Place:** Real de Catorce, San Luis Potosi
Last Foreign Residence: N.A.
Married to: N.A.   **Date:** N.A.
Where: N.A.
Crossed the Border on: 1887
Where: Laredo, Texas **Mode of travel:** N.A.
Date Certificate Issued: March 4, 1906
Alien Registration: N.A.
Description: N.A.

NATURALIZATION EXTRACTS

Name: Celestino Esquibel
District Court: County Court, County of Maverick, Eagle Pass, Texas
Address: N.A.
Type of Record: Declaration of Intention
DOB: N.A. (36 years old)   **Place:** Cuatro Cienegas, Coahuila
Last Foreign Residence: N.A.
Married to: N.A.   **Date:** N.A.
Where: N.A.
Crossed the Border on: 1859
Where: Eagle Pass, Texas   **Mode of travel:** N.A.
Date Certificate Issued: November 5, 1892
Alien Registration: N.A.
Description: N.A.

NATURALIZATION EXTRACTS

Name: Felipe Esquivel
District Court: County Court, County of Webb, Laredo, Texas
Address: N.A.
Type of Record: Declaration of Intention
DOB: N.A. (35 years old) **Place:** Victoria, Tamaulipas
Last Foreign Residence: N.A.
Married to: N.A.   **Date:** N.A.
Where: N.A.
Crossed the Border on: July 15, 1882
Where: Laredo, Texas **Mode of travel:** N.A.
Date Certificate Issued: November 7, 1892
Alien Registration: N.A.
Description: N.A.

NATURALIZATION EXTRACTS

Name: Ramon O. Felin
District Court: County Court, County of Webb, Laredo, Texas **Address:** N.A.
Type of Record: Declaration of Intention
DOB: N.A. (45 years old) **Place:** Mexico City, Mexico
Last Foreign Residence: N.A.
Married to: N.A.　　　　**Date:** N.A.
Where: N.A.
Crossed the Border on: December 17, 1892
Where: Laredo, Texas **Mode of travel:** N.A.
Date Certificate Issued: December 22, 1892
Alien Registration: N.A.
Description: N.A.

NATURALIZATION EXTRACTS

Name: Lorenzo Reyes Felix, Jr.
District Court: District Court, Los Angeles, California
Address: 2112 Crystal St., Los Angeles, California
Type of Record: Petition for Naturalization, No. 68576 (472098)   **DOB:** Nov. 14, 1909   **Place:** Quiriego, Sonora
Last Foreign Residence: Mexico City, Distrito Federal
Married to: Doris Rodehaver Felix   **Date:** July 17, 1937
Where: Los Angeles, California (Doris was born in Santa Barbara, California, on December 18, 1908.)   **Crossed the Border on:** January 5, 1929 (Crossed under the name of Lorenzo Felix-Valenzuela)   **Where:** Nogales, Arizona   **Mode of travel:** Afoot (Certificate of Arrival, No. 23-71124)   **Date Certificate Issued:** October 4, 1939
Alien Registration: N.A.
Description: Occupation: Musician. One Child listed – born in 1938.

NATURALIZATION EXTRACTS

Name: Gustavo Perez Figueroa
District Court: County Court, County of Webb, Laredo, Texas
Address: N.A.
Type of Record: Declaration of Intention
DOB: N.A. (29 years old) **Place:** Oaxaca, Mexico
Last Foreign Residence: N.A.
Married to: N.A.   **Date:** N.A.
Where: N.A.
Crossed the Border on: December 1905
Where: Laredo, Texas   **Mode of travel:** N.A.
Date Certificate Issued: June 25, 1906
Alien Registration: N.A.
Description: N.A.

NATURALIZATION EXTRACTS

Name: Jose Edward Frias
District Court: District Court, Los Angeles, California
Address: 4319 Fisher St., Los Angeles, California
Type of Record: Petition for Naturalization, No. 70988 (No. 695996)   **DOB:** March 19, 1914 **Place:** Torreon, Coahuila
Last Foreign Residence: Torreon, Coahuila
Married to: Not married   **Date:** N.A.
Where: N.A.
Crossed the Border on: April 17, 1914
Where: El Paso, Texas   **Mode of travel:** El Paso Electric Railway (Certificate of Arrival, No. 23-50645)   **Date Certificate Issued:** January 8, 1940 (Declaration of Intention 77373 filed on Aug. 22, 1936 in District Court, Los Angeles, California)   **Alien Registration:** N.A.
Description: Occupation: Merchant.

NATURALIZATION EXTRACTS

Name: Jesus Villegas Fuentes
District Court: District Court, Southern District of California, Los Angeles, California **Address:** 3611 Boundary Ave., Los Angeles, California
Type of Record: Declaration of Intention
DOB: Feb. 2, 1907 **Place:** Penjamo, Guanajuato
Last Foreign Residence: Irapuato, Guanajuato
Married to: Concepcion **Date:** September 10, 1929
Where: Los Angeles, California (Concepcion was born at Dolores Hidalgo, Guanajuato, on Dec. 8, 1911. She entered the U.S. at Laredo, Texas, on Nov. 29, 1920.) **Crossed the Border on:** July 15, 1916
Where: El Paso, Texas **Mode of travel:** Foot (Certificate of Arrival, No. 23-R113979) **Date Certificate Issued:** August 7, 1945
Alien Registration: N.A.
Description: Occupation: Laborer. Dark Complexion, 5 Feet, 3 Inches, Brown Eyes, Black Hair, 190 Pounds. Three children listed – born between 1934 and 1938.

NATURALIZATION EXTRACTS

Name: Secundino Fuentez
District Court: District Court, Los Angeles, California
Address: 4144 Floral Dr., Los Angeles, California (4148 Ficher St., Los Angeles, in the Declaration of Intention) **Type of Record:** Petition for Naturalization, No. 70907 (No. 695948) **DOB:** Jan. 7, 1902 **Place:** Silao, Guanajuato
Last Foreign Residence: Juarez, Chihuahua
Married to: Maria Luisa **Date:** January 5, 1935
Where: Santa Ana, California (Maria was born at Magdalena, Sonora, on Dec. 8, 1906. She entered the U.S. at Nogales, Arizona, on June 6, 1923.)
Crossed the Border on: December 24, 1920 (Crossed under the name of Secundino Fuentes)
Where: El Paso, Texas **Mode of travel:** El Paso Electric Railway (Certificate of Arrival, No. 23-16301)
Date Certificate Issued: January 5, 1940 (Declaration of Intention 81293 (No. 81293) filed May 25, 1937 in District Court, Los Angeles.)
Alien Registration: N.A.
Description: Occupation: Electrical helper. Dark Complexion, Dark Brown Eyes, Black Hair, 5 Feet, 2 Inches, 130 Pounds. Two children listed – born in 1927 and 1928.

NATURALIZATION EXTRACTS

Name: Angelo Padron Garcia

District Court: District Court, Southern District of California, Los Angeles, California   **Address:** 128 E. 27th St., Los Angeles, California

Type of Record: Declaration of Intention

DOB: Oct. 2, 1911 **Place:** Durango, Mexico

Last Foreign Residence: Durango, Mexico

Married to: Lily   **Date:** February 15, 1942

Where: Los Angeles, California (Lily was born in El Paso, Texas, date unknown.)   **Crossed the Border on:** May 5, 1917 (Crossed under the name of Angel Garcia)   **Where:** El Paso, Texas   **Mode of travel:** On foot (Certificate of Arrival, No. 23-100129)   **Date Certificate Issued:** July 14, 1945

Alien Registration: N.A.

Description: Occupation: Foundry worker. Dark Complexion, 5 Feet, 9½ Inches, 190 Pounds, Black Hair, Black Eyes.

NATURALIZATION EXTRACTS

Name: Antonia Ballin Garcia
District Court: District Court, Southern District of California, Los Angeles, California **Address:** 1047 S. Rowan Ave., Los Angeles, California
Type of Record: Declaration of Intention, No. 124513
DOB: Dec. 18, 1913 **Place:** Aguascalientes, Mexico
Last Foreign Residence: Aguascalientes, Mexico
Married to: Barbarito **Date:** Dec. 26, 1931
Where: Los Angeles, California (Barbarito was born at Cusivirachi, Chihuahua, on Dec. 4, 1910. He entered the U.S. at El Paso, Texas, in July 1911.)
Crossed the Border on: September 8, 1916 (Crossed under the name of Antonia Bagin (Ballin))
Where: El Paso, Texas **Mode of travel:** El Paso Electric Railroad (Certificate of Arrival, No. 23-133120)
Date Certificate Issued: July 16, 1945
Alien Registration: N.A.
Description: Occupation: Housewife. Medium Complexion, 4 Feet, 11½ Inches, 131 Pounds, Dark Brown Hair, Brown Eyes. Four children listed – all born between 1933 and 1941.

NATURALIZATION EXTRACTS

Name: Carlos Mateo Garcia aka Charles Mathew Garcia
District Court: District Court, Topeka, Kansas
Address: 209 East Carrillo St. Santa Barbra, Santa Barbara, California **Type of Record:** Petition for Naturalization
DOB: Sept. 21, 1914 **Place:** Zacatecas, Mexico
Last Foreign Residence: N.A.
Married to: Not married **Date:** N.A.
Where: N.A.
Crossed the Border on: September 20, 1920
Where: El Paso, Texas   **Mode of travel:** El Paso Electric Railway **Date Certificate Issued:** April 15, 1945
Alien Registration: N.A.
Description: Dark Complexion, 5 Feet, 6 Inches, 155 Pounds, Black Hair, Brown Eyes. Entered the U.S. Air Force on Feb. 19, 1942 under file No. 39019901 (Private First Class).

NATURALIZATION EXTRACTS

Name: Cresencion Garcia
District Court: County Court, County of Maverick, Eagle Pass, Texas   **Address:** N.A.
Type of Record: Declaration of Intention
DOB: N.A. (26 years old) **Place:** Saltillo, Coahuila
Last Foreign Residence: N.A.
Married to: N.A.   **Date:** N.A.
Where: N.A.
Crossed the Border on: November 3, 1883
Where: Eagle Pass, Texas   **Mode of travel:** N.A.
Date Certificate Issued: November 3, 1884
Alien Registration: N.A.
Description: N.A.

NATURALIZATION EXTRACTS

Name: Estanislado Garcia
District Court: County Court, County of Webb, Laredo, Texas **Address:** N.A.
Type of Record: Declaration of Intention
DOB: N.A. (40 years old) **Place:** Tula, Mexico
Last Foreign Residence: N.A.
Married to: N.A.   **Date:** N.A.
Where: N.A.
Crossed the Border on: November 16, 1874
Where: Laredo, Texas **Mode of travel:** N.A.
Date Certificate Issued: November 22, 1886
Alien Registration: N.A.
Description: N.A.

NATURALIZATION EXTRACTS

Name: Eugenio Garcia
District Court: District Court, Southern District of California, Los Angeles, California **Address:** 1463½ Ricardo St., Los Angeles, California
Type of Record: Declaration of Intention
DOB: Nov. 15, 1888 **Place:** Cuatro Cienegas, Coahuila
Last Foreign Residence: Villahomada, Mexico
Married to: Ventura **Date:** January 15, 1944
Where: Los Angeles, California (Ventura was born in Hacienda de Jolpa, Mexico, on July 14, 1889. She entered the U.S. at El Paso, Texas, in March 1924.) **Crossed the Border on:** June 25, 1903
Where: El Paso, Texas **Mode of travel:** On foot
Date Certificate Issued: July 16, 1945
Alien Registration: N.A.
Description: Occupation: Laborer. Medium Complexion, 5 Feet, 5 Inches, 166 Pounds, Black Hair, Brown Eyes. One child listed – born in 1918.

NATURALIZATION EXTRACTS

Name: Febronio Garcia aka Henry Garcia
District Court: District Court, Southern District of California, Los Angeles, California **Address:** 3536 Baswick St., Los Angeles, California
Type of Record: Declaration of Intention
DOB: June 23, 1905 **Place:** Huanimaro, Guanajuato
Last Foreign Residence: Huanimaro, Guanajuato
Married to: Mary   **Date:** Dec. 20, 1925
Where: Los Angeles, California (Mary was born at Uruapan, Michoacan, on June 10, 1909. She entered the U.S. at El Paso, Texas, on September 1, 1918.)
Crossed the Border on: August 16, 1907 (Crossed under the name of Febronio Garcia)
Where: El Paso, Texas   **Mode of travel:** On foot (Certificate of Arrival, No. 23-94391)
Date Certificate Issued: July 16, 1945
Alien Registration: N.A.
Description: Occupation: Journeyman. Dark Complexion, 5 Feet, 5 Inches, 145 Pounds, Black Hair, Brown Eyes. Two children listed – born in 1924 and 1926.

NATURALIZATION EXTRACTS

Name: Francisco Garcia
District Court: County Court, County of Maverick, Eagle Pass, Texas **Address:** N.A.
Type of Record: Declaration of Intention
DOB: N.A. (25 years old)　　**Place:** Cuatro Cienegas, Coahuila **Last Foreign Residence:** N.A.
Married to: N.A.　　　　**Date:** N.A.
Where: N.A.
Crossed the Border on: May 20, 1869
Where: Eagle Pass, Texas　**Mode of travel:** N.A.
Date Certificate Issued: October 14, 1886
Alien Registration: N.A.
Description: N.A.

NATURALIZATION EXTRACTS

Name: Gorgonio Garcia
District Court: County Court, County of Webb, Laredo, Texas **Address:** N.A.
Type of Record: Declaration of Intention, No. #1899
DOB: N.A. (26 years old) **Place:** Saltillo, Coahuila
Last Foreign Residence: N.A.
Married to: N.A.   **Date:** N.A.
Where: N.A.
Crossed the Border on: April 3, 1885
Where: Carbon City, Texas **Mode of travel:** N.A.
Date Certificate Issued: October 30, 1886
Alien Registration: N.A.
Description: N.A.

NATURALIZATION EXTRACTS

Name: Jose Maria Garcia
District Court: District Court, Topeka, Kansas
Address: 229 Hancock, Topeka, Kansas
Type of Record: Petition for Naturalization, No. 403214
DOB: Oct. 18, 1900   **Place:** Jerez, Zacatecas
Last Foreign Residence: Torreon, Coahuila
Married to: Rose Garcia   **Date:** June 1, 1927
Where: Topeka, Kansas (Rose was born Aug. 18, 1908 at Phillips, Oklahoma.)
Crossed the Border on: November 15, 1919
Where: El Paso, Texas   **Mode of travel:** El Paso Electric Railway (Certificate of Arrival, No. 15-3294)
Date Certificate Issued: August 20, 1940 (Declaration of Intention filed on April 15, 1935 at District Court, Topeka, Kansas.)
Alien Registration: N.A.
Description: Occupation: Machinist helper. Four children listed – born between 1928 and 1936.

NATURALIZATION EXTRACTS

Name: Luz Velasquez Garcia
District Court: District Court, District of Colorado, Denver, Colorado
Address: 928 20th Street, Denver, Colorado
Type of Record: Declaration of Intention, No. 14766 (21602)
DOB: March 2, 1909   **Place:** Jaralillo, Guanajuato
Last Foreign Residence: Jaralillo, Guanajuato
Married to: Manuel Tamayo Garcia   **Date:** Mar. 8, 1932
Where: Dallas, Texas (Manuel was born at Pueblo de Hayo, Jalisco, on March 21, 1902. He entered the U.S. at Presidio, Texas, on June 1, 1914.)
Crossed the Border on: June 30, 1916 (Crossed under the name of Luz Velasquez)
Where: Laredo, Texas   **Mode of travel:** Canoe (Certificate of Arrival, No. 1103-K-843)
Date Certificate Issued: April 9, 1947
Alien Registration: N.A.
Description: Occupation: Machine Operator. Dark complexion, 5 Feet, 4 Inches, 152 Pounds, Black-Grey Hair, Brown Eyes.

108

NATURALIZATION EXTRACTS

Name: Manuel Tamayo Garcia
District Court: District Court, District of Colorado, Denver, Colorado   **Address:** 928 20th Street, Denver, Colorado
Type of Record: Declaration of Intention, No. 14713
DOB: March 21, 1902   **Place:** Pueblo de Hayo, Jalisco
Last Foreign Residence: Ojinaga, Chihuahua
Married to: Luz Velasquez Garcia   **Date:** March 8, 1932
Where: Dallas, Texas (Luz was born at Jaralillo, Guanajuato, on March 2, 1909. She entered the U.S. on June 30, 1916 at Laredo, Texas.)   **Crossed the Border on:** June 1, 1904
Where: Presidio, Texas   **Mode of travel:** Boat (Certificate of Arrival, No. 1103-K-487 R)   **Date Certificate Issued:** October 9, 1946
Alien Registration: N.A.
Description: Occupation: Cook. Dark complexion, 5 Feet, 9 Inches, 215 Pounds, Black Hair, Brown Eyes. One child list – born in 1929.

NATURALIZATION EXTRACTS

Name: Marcelos Garza
District Court: County Court, County of Webb, Laredo, Texas **Address:** N.A.
Type of Record: Declaration of Intention, No. #1904
DOB: N.A. (25 years old) **Place:** Villaldama, Nuevo Leon
Last Foreign Residence: N.A.
Married to: N.A.   **Date:** N.A.
Where: N.A.
Crossed the Border on: September 16, 1885
Where: Laredo, Texas **Mode of travel:** N.A.
Date Certificate Issued: October 30, 1886
Alien Registration: N.A.
Description: N.A.

NATURALIZATION EXTRACTS

Name: Vatazar Garza
District Court: County Court, County of Maverick, Eagle Pass, Texas **Address:** N.A.
Type of Record: Declaration of Intention
DOB: N.A. (27 years old)   **Place:** Cuatro Cienegas, Coahuila **Last Foreign Residence:** N.A.
Married to: N.A.   **Date:** N.A.
Where: N.A.
Crossed the Border on: October 1891
Where: Eagle Pass, Texas   **Mode of travel:** N.A.
Date Certificate Issued: November 7, 1892
Alien Registration: N.A.
Description: N.A.

NATURALIZATION EXTRACTS

Name: Vidal Garza	
District Court: County Court, County of Webb, Laredo, Texas	
Address: N.A.	
Type of Record: Declaration of Intention, No. #2024	
DOB: N.A. (38 years old) **Place:** Montemorelos, Nuevo Leon	
Last Foreign Residence: N.A.	
Married to: N.A. **Date:** N.A.	
Where: N.A.	
Crossed the Border on: 1862	
Where: Laredo, Texas **Mode of travel:** N.A.	
Date Certificate Issued: November 1, 1886	
Alien Registration: N.A.	
Description: N.A.	

NATURALIZATION EXTRACTS

Name: Jose Gastlelum

District Court: Superior Court, Cochise County, State of Arizona **Address:** 805 "G" Avenue, Douglas, Arizona

Type of Record: Declaration of Intention, No. 898 (107405) **DOB:** April 11, 1894 **Place:** Sinaloa, Mexico

Last Foreign Residence: Al Fuerte, Sinaloa

Married to: N.A.   **Date:** N.A.

Where: N.A.

Crossed the Border on: April 1, 1900

Where: Nogales, Arizona   **Mode of travel:** Walked across.
Date Certificate Issued: August 31, 1916. Naturalization Certificate issued July 14, 1923: Authority dated July 7, 1923.
Alien Registration: N.A.

Description: Occupation: Proprietor, Pool Hall. Dark Complexion, 5 Feet, 9 Inches, 125 Pounds, Black Hair, Brown Eyes.

NATURALIZATION EXTRACTS

Name: Adalberto de la Pena Gomez
District Court: District Court, District of Colorado, Denver, Colorado **Address:** Denver General Hospital, Denver, Colorado
Type of Record: Declaration of Intention, No. 14670
DOB: Dec. 21, 1919   **Place:** Pachuca, Hidalgo
Last Foreign Residence: Mexico City, Mexico
Married to: Not married   **Date:** N.A.
Where: N.A.
Crossed the Border on: January 26, 1946 (Crossed under the name of Adalberto de la Pena y Gomez) **Where:** Laredo, Texas   **Mode of travel:** Laredo Bridge Company (Certificate of Arrival, No. 1103-K-49) **Date Certificate Issued:** April 17, 1946
Alien Registration: N.A.
Description: Occupation: Physician. Dark complexion, 5 Feet, 11 Inches, 160 Pounds, Black Hair, Blue Eyes.

NATURALIZATION EXTRACTS

Name: Albino Gomez
District Court: County Court, County of Maverick, Eagle Pass, Texas   **Address:** N.A.
Type of Record: Declaration of Intention
DOB: N.A. (59 years old)   **Place:** Parras, Coahuila
Last Foreign Residence: N.A.
Married to: N.A.   **Date:** N.A.
Where: N.A.
Crossed the Border on: May 1, 1882
Where: Eagle Pass, Texas   **Mode of travel:** N.A.
Date Certificate Issued: October 25, 1886
Alien Registration: N.A.
Description: N.A.

NATURALIZATION EXTRACTS

Name: Feliciano Gomez
District Court: Superior Court, Cochise County, State of Arizona **Address:** Bisbee, Arizona
Type of Record: Declaration of Intention, No. 715 (97555)
DOB: April 1876 **Place:** Llagualica (Yahualica ?), Guadalajara, Jalisco **Last Foreign Residence:** Cananea, Sonora
Married to: N.A.   **Date:** N.A.
Where: N.A.
Crossed the Border on: August 4, 1904
Where: Nogales, Arizona   **Mode of travel:** Sonora Railroad **Date Certificate Issued:** December 9, 1914
Alien Registration: N.A.
Description: Occupation: Laborer. Dark Complexion, 5 Feet, 3 Inches, 154 Pounds, Black Hair, Brown Eyes.

NATURALIZATION EXTRACTS

Name: Rafael Romo Gomez
District Court: District Court, District of Colorado, Denver, Colorado   **Address:** 2141 Larimer, Denver, Colorado
Type of Record: Declaration of Intention, No. 14487 (20771)   **DOB:** Aug. 30, 1890 **Place:** Zacatecas, Zacatecas
Last Foreign Residence: Ojocaliente, Zacatecas
Married to: Maria de Jesus M. de Gomez   **Date:** October 19, 1924   **Where:** Denver, Colorado (Maria was born at Jerez, Zacatecas on Jan. 1, 1893. She entered the U.S. at El Paso, Texas, on October 5, 1921.)
Crossed the Border on: July 15, 1918 (Crossed under the name of Rafael Gomez)
Where: Laredo, Texas **Mode of travel:** Footbridge (Certificate of Arrival, No. 18-13503)
Date Certificate Issued: August 5, 1943
Alien Registration: N.A.
Description: Occupation: Merchant. 6 Feet, 1 Inch, 140 Pounds, Brown Hair, Brown Eyes.

NATURALIZATION EXTRACTS

Name: Juan Gonzales

District Court: County Court, County of Webb, Laredo, Texas
Address: N.A.

Type of Record: Declaration of Intention

DOB: N.A. (65 years old) **Place:** Candela, Coahuila

Last Foreign Residence: N.A.

Married to: N.A.   **Date:** N.A.

Where: N.A.

Crossed the Border on: May 20, 1894

Where: Laredo, Texas **Mode of travel:** N.A.

Date Certificate Issued: January 27, 1906

Alien Registration: N.A.

Description: N.A.

NATURALIZATION EXTRACTS

Name: Juan Gonzales
District Court: County Court, County of Maverick, Eagle Pass, Texas   **Address:** N.A.
Type of Record: Declaration of Intention
DOB: N.A. (24 years old) **Place:** Saltillo, Coahuila
Last Foreign Residence: N.A.
Married to: N.A. **Date:** N.A.
Where: N.A.
Crossed the Border on: Winter 1888
Where: Eagle Pass, Texas **Mode of travel:** N.A.
Date Certificate Issued: November 7, 1892
Alien Registration: N.A.
Description: N.A.

NATURALIZATION EXTRACTS

Name: Maximiliano Gonzales
District Court: County Court, County of Maverick, Eagle Pass, Texas **Address:** N.A.
Type of Record: Declaration of Intention
DOB: N.A. (22 years old)   **Place:** Monclova, Coahuila
Last Foreign Residence: N.A.
Married to: N.A.   **Date:** N.A.
Where: N.A.
Crossed the Border on: September 1, 1886
Where: Eagle Pass, Texas   **Mode of travel:** N.A.
Date Certificate Issued: October 15, 1886
Alien Registration: N.A.
Description: N.A.

NATURALIZATION EXTRACTS

Name: Yndalecio Gonzales	

District Court: County Court, County of Maverick, Eagle Pass, Texas

Address: N.A.

Type of Record: Declaration of Intention

DOB: N.A. (28 years old)　　**Place:** Monclova, Coahuila

Last Foreign Residence: N.A.

Married to: N.A.　　　　**Date:** N.A.

Where: N.A.

Crossed the Border on: September 16, 1884

Where: Laredo, Texas　**Mode of travel:** N.A.

Date Certificate Issued: February 17, 1906

Alien Registration: N.A.

Description: N.A.

NATURALIZATION EXTRACTS

Name: Ana Gonzalez
District Court: District Court, Ft. Scott, Kansas
Address: Fredonia, Wilson County, Kansas
Type of Record: Declaration of Intention
DOB: Jan. 1, 1919   **Place:** Zacapu, Michoacan
Last Foreign Residence: Zacapu, Michoacan
Married to: N.A.   **Date:** N.A.
Where: N.A.
Crossed the Border on: April 18, 1920
Where: El Paso, Texas   **Mode of travel:** Railroad
Date Certificate Issued: July 22, 1944
Alien Registration: N.A.
Description: Occupation: Printing shop employee. Olive Complexion, Brown Eyes, Brown Hair, 5 Feet, 4 Inches, 134 Pounds. Four children listed – all born between 1915 and 1924.

NATURALIZATION EXTRACTS

Name: Emiliano Gonzalez
District Court: District Court, Los Angeles, California
Address: 910 Adobe St., Los Angeles, California
Type of Record: Petition for Naturalization, No. 70918 (No. 695861)   **DOB:** April 15, 1888 **Place:** Chihuahua, Chihuahua
Last Foreign Residence: Chihuahua, Chihuahua
Married to: Trinidad   **Date:** June 3, 1913
Where: Chihuahua, Mexico (Trinidad was born at Bisbee, Arizona, on May 23, 1883.)   **Crossed the Border on:** February 26, 1920
Where: El Paso, Texas   **Mode of travel:** El Paso Electric Railway (Certificate of Arrival, No. 23-30548)
Date Certificate Issued: January 5, 1940 (Declaration of Intention 64593 (No. 99261) filed on Feb. 19, 1934 in District Court, Los Angeles, California.)
Alien Registration: N.A.
Description: Occupation: Boiler Maker – Laborer. Dark Complexion, Brown Eyes, Brown Hair, 5 Feet, 6 Inches, 157 Pounds. One child listed – born in 1909.

NATURALIZATION EXTRACTS

Name: Juan Baldez Gonzalez
District Court: District Court, Los Angeles, California
Address: 1066 S. Soto St., Los Angeles, California
Type of Record: Petition for Naturalization, No. 71039 (No. 69528)
DOB: June 24, 1875 **Place:** Santa Rosalia, Mexico
Last Foreign Residence: Sausillo, Mexico
Married to: Clemencia   **Date:** May 5, 1909
Where: Del Rio, Texas (Clemencia was born in Del Rio, Texas, on March 20, 1892.)
Crossed the Border on: August 15, 1893
Where: El Paso, Texas   **Mode of travel:** Railway
Date Certificate Issued: January 11, 1940 (Declaration of Intention 83122 filed on Oct. 22, 1937 in District Court, Los Angeles, California.)
Alien Registration: N.A.
Description: Occupation: Laborer. Six children listed – all born between 1916 and 1930. Resided in Los Angeles County since 1917.

NATURALIZATION EXTRACTS

Name: Leonardo Gonzalez
District Court: County Court, County of Maverick, Eagle Pass, Texas   **Address:** N.A.
Type of Record: Declaration of Intention
DOB: N.A. (34 years old)　　**Place:** Monclova, Coahuila
Last Foreign Residence: N.A.
Married to: N.A.　　　　**Date:** N.A.
Where: N.A.
Crossed the Border on: November 14, 1895
Where: Eagle Pass, Texas　**Mode of travel:** N.A.
Date Certificate Issued: December 31, 1895
Alien Registration: N.A.
Description: N.A.

NATURALIZATION EXTRACTS

Name: Manuel Parra Gonzalez
District Court: District Court, Southern District of California, Los Angeles, California **Address:** 2121 N. Eastern Ave., Los Angeles, California
Type of Record: Declaration of Intention
DOB: June 17, 1904 **Place:** Casas Grandes, Chihuahua
Last Foreign Residence: Casas Grandes, Chihuahua
Married to: Not married   **Date:** N.A.
Where: N.A.
Crossed the Border on: March 31, 1909 (Crossed the border under the name of Manuel Gonzalez) **Where:** El Paso, Texas   **Mode of travel:** El Paso Electric Railroad (Certificate of Arrival, No. 23-133639) **Date Certificate Issued:** July 21, 1945
Alien Registration: N.A.
Description: Occupation: Auto Park Ens. Dark Complexion, 5 Feet, 11 Inches, 160 Pounds, Black Hair, Blue Eyes.

NATURALIZATION EXTRACTS

Name: Maria Sanchez de Gonzalez
District Court: District Court, Southern District of California, Los Angeles, California **Address:** 124 Norman Court, Los Angeles, California
Type of Record: Declaration of Intention, No. 123788
DOB: Nov. 2, 1908 **Place:** Guadalupe, Mexico
Last Foreign Residence: Juarez, Chihuahua
Married to: Indalecio **Date:** January 16, 1928
Where: Santa Ana, California (Indalecio was born in Guadalupe, Mexico, on April 29, 1904. He entered the U.S. at El Paso, Texas, on Feb. 4, 1925.)
Crossed the Border on: January 7, 1924 (Crossed under the name of Maria Sanchez)
Where: El Paso, Texas **Mode of travel:** El Paso Electric Railway (Certificate of Arrival, No. 23-132211)
Date Certificate Issued: February 26, 1945
Alien Registration: N.A.
Description: Occupation: Housewife. Medium Complexion, 5 Feet, 2 Inches, Brown Eyes, Black Hair, 128 Pounds. Three children listed – born in 1928 and 1933.

NATURALIZATION EXTRACTS

Name: Serapio Gonzalez
District Court: County Court, County of Maverick, Eagle Pass, Texas   **Address:** N.A.
Type of Record: Declaration of Intention
DOB: N.A. (47 years old)　　**Place:** Nuevo Laredo, Tamaulipas   **Last Foreign Residence:** N.A.
Married to: N.A.　　**Date:** N.A.
Where: N.A.
Crossed the Border on: January 15, 1880
Where: Laredo, Texas　**Mode of travel:** N.A.
Date Certificate Issued: October 14, 1886
Alien Registration: N.A.
Description: N.A.

Name: Camilo Hernandez
District Court: County Court, County of Webb, Laredo, Texas **Address:** N.A.
Type of Record: Declaration of Intention, No. #1908
DOB: N.A. (42 years old) **Place:** Linares, Nuevo Leon
Last Foreign Residence: N.A.
Married to: N.A.   **Date:** N.A.
Where: N.A.
Crossed the Border on: October 1885
Where: Laredo, Texas   **Mode of travel:** N.A.
Date Certificate Issued: October 29, 1886
Alien Registration: N.A.
Description: N.A.

NATURALIZATION EXTRACTS

Name: Georgonio Hernandez
District Court: District Court, Ft. Scott, Kansas
Address: Roper, Wilson County, Kansas
Type of Record: Declaration of Intention
DOB: Dec. 9, 1892   **Place:** Leon, Guanajuato
Last Foreign Residence: Leon, Guanajuato
Married to: Luz Hernandez   **Date:** June 1914
Where: Leon, Guanajuato (Luz was born at Leon, Guanajuato, on June 15, 1898. She entered the U.S. at Laredo, Texas, in October 1916.) **Crossed the Border on:** December 26, 1916
Where: Laredo, Texas   **Mode of travel:** Footbridge
Date Certificate Issued: July 6, 1931
Alien Registration: N.A.
Description: Occupation: Foreman, M.O.P.R.R. Dark Complexion, Brown Eyes, Black Hair, 5 Feet, 6 Inches, 152 Pounds. Four children listed – all born between 1915 and 1924.

NATURALIZATION EXTRACTS

Name: Josephine Hernandez
District Court: District Court, District of Colorado, Denver, Colorado   **Address:** 320 East 16th Ave., Denver, Colorado
Type of Record: Declaration of Intention, No. 14095
DOB: June 12, 1921   **Place:** San Ramon, Jalisco
Last Foreign Residence: San Ramon, Jalisco
Married to: Not married   **Date:** N.A.
Where: N.A.
Crossed the Border on: Jan. 20, 1922 (Crossed under the name of Josefina Hernandez)   **Where:** El Paso, Texas   **Mode of travel:** El Paso Electric Railway (Certificate of Arrival, No. 19-14423)   **Date Certificate Issued:** September 4, 1941
Alien Registration: N.A.
Description: Occupation: Secretarial work. Medium Complexion, 5 Feet, 2½ Inches, 114 Pounds, Black Hair, Brown Eyes.

NATURALIZATION EXTRACTS

Name: Sostenes Hernandez
District Court: County Court, County of Webb, Laredo, Texas **Address:** N.A.
Type of Record: Declaration of Intention, No. #1975
DOB: N.A. (53 years old) **Place:** Real de Charcas, Mexico **Last Foreign Residence:** N.A.
Married to: N.A. **Date:** N.A.
Where: N.A.
Crossed the Border on: March 12, 1866
Where: Laredo, Texas **Mode of travel:** N.A.
Date Certificate Issued: October 23, 1886
Alien Registration: N.A.
Description: N.A.

NATURALIZATION EXTRACTS

Name: Honorato Jimenez
District Court: District Court, Los Angeles, California
Address: 1301 W. 48th St., Los Angeles, California
Type of Record: Petition for Naturalization, No. 71030
DOB: Jan. 16, 1891 **Place:** Guadalajara, Jalisco
Last Foreign Residence: San Luis Potosi, Mexico
Married to: Carmen **Date:** April 7, 1915
Where: Los Angeles, California (Carmen was born at Merced Falls, California, on Oct. 12, 1888.)   **Crossed the Border on:** July 8, 1898
Where: El Paso, Texas **Mode of travel:** Mexican Central Railroad
Date Certificate Issued: January 9, 1940 (Declaration of Intention 72210 filed June 29, 1935 in District Court, Los Angeles, California)
Alien Registration: N.A.
Description: Occupation: Field Meter Inspector. Two children listed – born in 1916 and 1930. Wife Carmen was naturalized on Oct. 11, 1935 in District Court, Los Angeles (Certificate No. 4061357).

NATURALIZATION EXTRACTS

Name: Elena Salazar Joers
District Court: District Court, Los Angeles, California
Address: 1753 S. Corning St., Los Angeles, California
Type of Record: Petition for Naturalization, No. 688340 (472223)   **DOB:** Aug. 18, 1908 **Place:** Alamos, Sonora
Last Foreign Residence: Magdalena, Sonora
Married to: Fred Joers **Date:** February 5, 1938
Where: Santa Ana, California (Fred was born in Xilitla, Mexico, on Dec. 31, 1905. He entered the U.S. at El Paso, Texas, in July 1910.)   **Crossed the Border on:** July 11, 1928 (Crossed the border under the name of Elena Salazar-Erbe)   **Where:** Nogales, Arizona **Mode of travel:** Afoot (Certificate of Arrival, No. 23-70133)   **Date Certificate Issued:** September 26, 1939
Alien Registration: N.A.
Description: Occupation: Sewing Operator.

NATURALIZATION EXTRACTS

Name: Serapio Juarez
District Court: County Court, County of Webb, Laredo, Texas   **Address:** N.A.
Type of Record: Declaration of Intention
DOB: N.A. (58 years old) **Place:** Cadereyta, Nuevo Leon
Last Foreign Residence: N.A.
Married to: N.A.   **Date:** N.A.
Where: N.A.
Crossed the Border on: July 16, 1875
Where: Laredo, Texas **Mode of travel:** N.A.
Date Certificate Issued: November 1, 1890
Alien Registration: N.A.
Description: N.A.

NATURALIZATION EXTRACTS

Name: Francisco Lagrange
District Court: County Court, County of Maverick, Eagle Pass, Texas
Address: N.A.
Type of Record: Declaration of Intention
DOB: N.A. (23 years old)   **Place:** Cuatros Cienegas, Coahuila
Last Foreign Residence: N.A.
Married to: N.A.   **Date:** N.A.
Where: N.A.
Crossed the Border on: December 1878
Where: Eagle Pass, Texas   **Mode of travel:** N.A.
Date Certificate Issued: October 25, 1883
Alien Registration: N.A.
Description: N.A.

NATURALIZATION EXTRACTS

Name: Leon Alberto Lancon
District Court: District Court, Los Angeles, California
Address: 428 E. 29th St., Los Angeles, California
Type of Record: Petition for Naturalization, No. 70816 (No. 691171)   **DOB:** Jan. 11, 1880   **Place:** Guadalupe, Zacatecas
Last Foreign Residence: Chihuahua, Mexico
Married to: Carlota Romero de Lancon   **Date:** March 11, 1912   **Where:** Chihuahua, Chihuahua (Carlota was born at Chihuahua, Chihuahua, on July 24, 1885. She entered the U.S. in 1912 at El Paso, Texas.)   **Crossed the Border on:** June 2, 1921
Where: San Ysidro, California   **Mode of travel:** Auto (Certificate of Arrival, No. 23-38512)   **Date Certificate Issued:** January 2, 1940 (Declaration of Intention 68611 (No. 14982) filed Jan. 14, 1935 in Circuit Court, Los Angeles.)   **Alien Registration:** N.A.   **Description:** Occupation: Janitor. Fair Complexion. Light Brown Eyes, Grayish Hair, 5 Feet, 7 Inches, 130 Pounds. Six children listed – all born between 1912 and 1924.

NATURALIZATION EXTRACTS

Name: Jose Sierras Leon
District Court: Superior Court, Cochise County, State of Arizona **Address:** Benson, Arizona
Type of Record: Declaration of Intention
DOB: Nov. 14, 1884   **Place:** Montazuma, Sonora
Last Foreign Residence: Arizpe, Sonora
Married to: N.A.   **Date:** N.A.
Where: N.A.
Crossed the Border on: August 1890
Where: Santa Cruz, Arizona   **Mode of travel:** Horseback
Date Certificate Issued: June 10, 1914
Alien Registration: N.A.
Description: Occupation: Cowman. Dark Complexion, 5 Feet, 9 Inches, 131 Pounds, Black Hair, Brown Eyes.

NATURALIZATION EXTRACTS

Name: Jesus Ernesto Limon
District Court: Superior Court, Cochise County, State of Arizona **Address:** General Delivery, Bisbee, Arizona
Type of Record: Declaration of Intention, No. 1098 (293455) **DOB:** Dec. 17, 1895   **Place:** Hermosillo, Sonora
Last Foreign Residence: Guaymas, Sonora
Married to: Teresa Rincon   **Date:** N.A.
Where: N.A. (Teresa was born at Bisbee, Arizona.)
Crossed the Border on: May 11, 1912
Where: Nogales, Arizona   **Mode of travel:** Railroad train – Southern Pacific of Mexico **Date Certificate Issued:** September 14, 1917
Alien Registration: N.A.
Description: Occupation: Miner. Dark Complexion, 5 Feet, 5 Inches, 130 Pounds, Black Hair, Brown Eyes.

NATURALIZATION EXTRACTS

Name: Felicita Gutierres de Lopes
District Court: District Court, District of Colorado, Denver, Colorado
Address: 1401 S. Acuna St., Denver, Colorado
Type of Record: Declaration of Intention, No. 14140 (19876)
DOB: August 3, 1879   **Place:** Calera, Zacatecas
Last Foreign Residence: Gomez Palacios, Durango
Married to: Pioquinto de Lopez   **Date:** October 1890
Where: Calera, Zacatecas (Pioquinto was born on May 5, 1876 in Lagos de Moreno, Jalisco. He entered the U.S. at El Paso, Texas, in 1907.)
Crossed the Border on: October 5, 1922
Where: El Paso, Texas   **Mode of travel:** El Paso Electric Railway (Certificate of Arrival, No. 19-13616)
Date Certificate Issued: October 22, 1941
Alien Registration: N.A.
Description: Occupation: Housewife. Dark complexion, 5 Feet, 0 Inches, 115 Pounds, Grey Hair, Brown Eyes. Four children listed – all born between 1902 and 1915.

NATURALIZATION EXTRACTS

Name: Pioquinto Lopes
District Court: District Court, District of Colorado, Denver, Colorado **Address:** 1401 S. Acuna St., Denver, Colorado
Type of Record: Declaration of Intention, No. 14117 (19855) **DOB:** May 5, 1876 **Place:** Lagos de Moreno, Jalisco
Last Foreign Residence: Gomez Palacios, Durango
Married to: Felicita Gutierrez Lopez **Date:** October 1890 **Where:** Calera, Zacatecas (Felicita was born on Aug. 3, 1879 in Calera, Zacatecas. She entered the U.S. at El Paso, Texas, on October 5, 1922.) **Crossed the Border on:** August 4, 1922
Where: El Paso, Texas **Mode of travel:** El Paso Electric Railway (Certificate of Arrival, No. 19-13619) **Date Certificate Issued:** October 7, 1941
Alien Registration: N.A.
Description: Occupation: Laborer. Dark complexion, 5 Feet, 3 Inches, 145 Pounds, Black Hair, Brown Eyes. Four children listed – all born between 1902 and 1915.

NATURALIZATION EXTRACTS

Name: Bartolo Lopez
District Court: County Court, County of Webb, Laredo, Texas **Address:** N.A.
Type of Record: Declaration of Intention
DOB: N.A. (22 years old) **Place:** Monterrey, Nuevo Leon
Last Foreign Residence: N.A.
Married to: N.A.   **Date:** N.A.
Where: N.A.
Crossed the Border on: May 20, 1885
Where: Laredo, Texas **Mode of travel:** N.A.
Date Certificate Issued: January 30, 1906
Alien Registration: N.A.
Description: N.A.

NATURALIZATION EXTRACTS

Name: Isabel Lopez
District Court: District Court, Los Angeles, California
Address: 697 N. Palos Verdes, San Pedro, California
Type of Record: Petition for Naturalization, No. 68334 (470833)   **DOB:** Dec. 14, 1898   **Place:** Zacatecas, Mexico
Last Foreign Residence: Nogales, Sonora
Married to: Theodoro P. Lopez   **Date:** Jan. 1, 1925
Where: Nogales, Arizona (Theodoro was born in Rosamond, Arizona, on Jan. 7, 1898.)   **Crossed the Border on:** July 31, 1922 (Crossed under the name of Isabel Montalvo)   **Where:** Nogales, Arizona   **Mode of travel:** On foot (Certificate of Arrival, No. 23-70128: #413/6046)   **Date Certificate Issued:** September 26, 1939
Alien Registration: N.A.
Description: Occupation: Housewife. One Child listed – born in 1936.

NATURALIZATION EXTRACTS

Name: Nepomuceno Lopez
District Court: County Court, County of Maverick, Eagle Pass, Texas **Address:** N.A.
Type of Record: Declaration of Intention
DOB: N.A. (43 years old)   **Place:** Santa Rosa, Mexico
Last Foreign Residence: N.A.
Married to: N.A.   **Date:** N.A.
Where: N.A.
Crossed the Border on: February 23, 1876
Where: Eagle Pass, Texas   **Mode of travel:** N.A.
Date Certificate Issued: November 6, 1882
Alien Registration: N.A.
Description: N.A.

NATURALIZATION EXTRACTS

Name: Raul Lopez
District Court: District Court, Los Angeles, California
Address: 623 8th St., San Pedro, California
Type of Record: Petition for Naturalization, No. 71167 (696560) **DOB:** Dec. 25, 1912 **Place:** Jimenez, Chihuahua
Last Foreign Residence: Juarez, Chihuahua
Married to: Magdalena Lopez **Date:** Feb. 28, 1937
Where: San Pedro, California (Magdalena was born at Snyder, Texas, on May 29, 1915.) **Crossed the Border on:** April 2, 1926
Where: El Paso, Texas **Mode of travel:** El Paso Electric Railroad (Certificate of Arrival, No. 23-71971) **Date Certificate Issued:** January 18, 1940
Alien Registration: N.A.
Description: Occupation: Cannery worker. One child listed – born in 1938. Wife is a citizen by birth.

NATURALIZATION EXTRACTS

Name: Juan Pablo Luna
District Court: County Court, County of Webb, Laredo, Texas **Address:** N.A.
Type of Record: Declaration of Intention, No. #1894
DOB: N.A. (34 years old) **Place:** Saltillo, Coahuila
Last Foreign Residence: N.A.
Married to: N.A.   **Date:** N.A.
Where: N.A.
Crossed the Border on: July 20, 1878
Where: Laredo, Texas **Mode of travel:** N.A.
Date Certificate Issued: October 30, 1886
Alien Registration: N.A.
Description: N.A.

NATURALIZATION EXTRACTS

Name: Ignacio Contreras Mackintosh
District Court: District Court, District of Colorado, Denver, Colorado **Address:** 3435 Lawrence St., Denver, Colorado
Type of Record: Declaration of Intention, No. 13036 (17994) **DOB:** July 16, 1896 **Place:** Guadalupe y Calvo, Chihuahua **Last Foreign Residence:** Chihuahua, Mexico
Married to: Carmen Yeramendi **Date:** June 19, 1919
Where: Juarez, Chihuahua (Carmen was born on Nov. 22, 1901 in Mexico City, Mexico. She entered the U.S. on February 1919 at El Paso, Texas.) **Crossed the Border on:** February 21, 1917 (Crossed under the name of Ignacio McIntosh y Contreras) **Where:** El Paso, Texas **Mode of travel:** El Paso Electric Railway (Certificate of Arrival, No. 18-11481) **Date Certificate Issued:** May 10, 1938
Alien Registration: N.A.
Description: Occupation: Printer. Race: Scottish. Nationality: Mexican. Medium complexion, 5 Feet, 7 Inches, 139 Pounds, Brown Hair, Brown Eyes. Eight children listed – all born between 1926 and 1937.

NATURALIZATION EXTRACTS

Name: Refugio Mancillas
District Court: District Court, Los Angeles, California
Address: 1122 E. Anaheim Blvd., Wilmington, California
Type of Record: Petition for Naturalization, No. 71087 (696186) **DOB:** Jan. 3, 1897   **Place:** Lagos de Moreno, Jalisco
Last Foreign Residence: Lagos, Mexico
Married to: Enriqueta Arrellanes   **Date:** Dec. 23, 1928
Where: Los Angeles, California (Enriqueta was born at Santa Rosalia, Mexico, on August 13, 1906. She entered the U.S. at El Paso, Texas, in 1910.)
Crossed the Border on: August 24, 1911 (Crossed under the name of Refugio Mancillo)
Where: Laredo, Texas   **Mode of travel:** Footbridge (Certificate of Arrival, No. 23-55416)
Date Certificate Issued: January 15, 1940 (Declaration of Intention 81491 (No. 47391) filed on June 19, 1937 in District Court, Los Angeles, California.)
Alien Registration: N.A.
Description: Occupation: Laborer. Dark Complexion, Brown Eyes, Black Hair, 5 Feet, 4 Inches, 130 Pounds. Two children listed – born in 1929 and 1931.

NATURALIZATION EXTRACTS

Name: Maria Paz Mac Manus
District Court: District Court, Southern District of California, Los Angeles, California **Address:** 2874 Edgehill Dr., Los Angeles, California
Type of Record: Declaration of Intention, No. 125741
DOB: Feb. 7, 1892 **Place:** Chautitlan, Estado de Mexico
Last Foreign Residence: Mexico City, Distrito Federal
Married to: Manuel (widowed) **Date:** Nov. 12, 1910
Where: Mexico City, Mexico (Manuel was born in Chihuahua, Mexico, on March 4, 1866. He entered the U.S. at Eagle Pass, Texas, on Feb. 18, 1916.)
Crossed the Border on: February 23, 1916 (Crossed under the name of Paz M. de McManus)
Where: Eagle Pass, Texas **Mode of travel:** Toll Bridge (Certificate of Arrival, No. 1600-K-1412)
Date Certificate Issued: April 19, 1946
Alien Registration: N.A.
Description: Occupation: Assembler-Clothing. Light Complexion, 5 Feet, 1 Inch, 110 Pounds, Brown/Gray Hair, Brown Eyes. Two children listed – born in 1911 and 1915.

NATURALIZATION EXTRACTS

Name: Susana Mac Manus
District Court: District Court, Southern District of California, Los Angeles, California **Address:** 2874 Edgehill Dr., Los Angeles, California
Type of Record: Declaration of Intention, No. 125739
DOB: Sept. 11, 1911 **Place:** Mexico City, Distrito Federal
Last Foreign Residence: Mexico City, Distrito Federal
Married to: Not married **Date:** N.A.
Where: N.A.
Crossed the Border on: February 23, 1916 (Crossed under the name of Susana McManus) **Where:** Eagle Pass, Texas **Mode of travel:** Toll Bridge (Certificate of Arrival, No. 1600-K-1930) **Date Certificate Issued:** April 19, 1946
Alien Registration: N.A.
Description: Occupation: Key-Punch Clerk. Fair Complexion, 5 Feet, 2 Inch, 97 Pounds, Dark Brown Hair, Hazel Eyes. .

NATURALIZATION EXTRACTS

Name: Angela Magallanes
District Court: District Court, Southern District of California, Los Angeles, California **Address:** 552 S. St. Louis St., Los Angeles, California
Type of Record: Declaration of Intention, No. 125774
DOB: Sept. 14, 1914 **Place:** Aguascalientes, Aguascalientes **Last Foreign Residence:** Aguascalientes, Aguascalientes
Married to: Not married   **Date:** N.A.
Where: N.A.
Crossed the Border on: April 5, 1923
Where: El Paso, Texas   **Mode of travel:** El Paso Electric Railway (Certificate of Arrival, No. 1600-K-2460) **Date Certificate Issued:** April 25, 1945
Alien Registration: N.A.
Description: Occupation: Sewing Machine Operator. Fair Complexion, 5 Feet, 0 Inches, 140 Pounds, Dark Brown Hair, Brown Eyes.

NATURALIZATION EXTRACTS

Name: Bernarda Montoya Magana
District Court: District Court, Southern District of California, Los Angeles, California   **Address:** 10902 Crossus Ave., Los Angeles, California
Type of Record: Declaration of Intention, No. 125771
DOB: Aug. 20, 1898   **Place:** Penjamo, Guanajuato
Last Foreign Residence: Penjamo, Guanajuato
Married to: Francisco   **Date:** March 9, 1917
Where: Los Angeles, California (Francisco was born on Oct. 4, 1895 in Mexico. He entered the U.S. at El Paso, Texas, in 1913. Now divorced.)
Crossed the Border on: August 5, 1910 (Crossed under the name of Bernarda Montoya)
Where: El Paso, Texas   **Mode of travel:** El Paso Electric Railway (Certificate of Arrival, No. 1600-K-2291)
Date Certificate Issued: April 25, 1945
Alien Registration: N.A.
Description: Occupation: Power Machine Operator. Dark Complexion, 5 Feet, 3 Inches, 150 Pounds, Black Hair, Brown Eyes. Four children listed – all born between 1917 and 1924.

NATURALIZATION EXTRACTS

Name: Tomas Maldonado
District Court: County Court, County of Maverick, Eagle Pass, Texas   **Address:** N.A.
Type of Record: Declaration of Intention
DOB: N.A. (27 years old) **Place:** Zaragoza, Coahuila
Last Foreign Residence: N.A.
Married to: N.A.   **Date:** N.A.
Where: N.A.
Crossed the Border on: January 1883
Where: Eagle Pass, Texas   **Mode of travel:** N.A.
Date Certificate Issued: November 1, 1884
Alien Registration: N.A.
Description: N.A.

NATURALIZATION EXTRACTS

Name: Jose Guzman Mapula
District Court: District Court, Southern District of California, Los Angeles, California   **Address:** 1615½ Michigan Ave., Los Angeles, California
Type of Record: Declaration of Intention
DOB: April 9, 1903 **Place:** Villa Corona, Durango
Last Foreign Residence: Tijuana, Baja California
Married to: Maria **Date:** June 10, 1939
Where: Los Angeles, California (Maria was born in Morcillo, Durango, in 1911. She entered the U.S. at San Ysidro, California, on Sept. 29, 1944.)   **Crossed the Border on:** Sept. 29, 1944
Where: San Ysidro, California **Mode of travel:** On foot (Certificate of Arrival, No. 23-132278)   **Date Certificate Issued:** April 4, 1945
Alien Registration: N.A.
Description: Occupation: Bus Boy. Medium Complexion, 5 Feet, 8 Inches, 140 Pounds, Black Hair, Brown Eyes. Two children listed – born in 1940 and 1942.

NATURALIZATION EXTRACTS

Name: Ramon Frescas Marquez aka Ray F. Marquez
District Court: U.S. Military Naturalization
Address: Serving in the military at Lichfield, Staffordshire, England, 347th Engineer Regiment **Type of Record:** Petition for Naturalization
DOB: March 17, 1915   **Place:** San Andres, Chihuahua
Last Foreign Residence: N.A.
Married to: N.A.   **Date:** N.A.
Where: N.A.
Crossed the Border on: 1918
Where: El Paso, Texas   **Mode of travel:** National Railways of Mexico **Date Certificate Issued:** May 14, 1943
Alien Registration: N.A.
Description: Technician Grade IV, Serial No. 39308764. Enlisted at Mulvane, Sedgwick County, Kansas. Dark Complexion, Brown Eyes, Brown Hair, 5 Feet, 4½ Inches, 130 Pounds.

NATURALIZATION EXTRACTS

Name: Helen Frances Rul Martin
District Court: District Court, Los Angeles, California
Address: 7415 Whitsett St., Los Angeles, California
Type of Record: Petition for Naturalization, No. 68336 (472225) **DOB:** June 19, 1917   **Place:** Mexico City, Mexico
Last Foreign Residence: Mexico City, Mexico
Married to: Willard Arthur Martin **Date:** Feb. 21, 1936
Where: Glendale, California (Willard was born in Croften, Nebraska, on Feb. 25, 1910.) **Crossed the Border on:** December 5, 1917 (Crossed the border under the name of Helen Rul) **Where:** Laredo, Texas   **Mode of travel:** Railroad Bridge (Certificate of Arrival, No. 23-70123) **Date Certificate Issued:** September 26, 1939
Alien Registration: N.A.
Description: Occupation: Housewife. One Child listed – born in 1938.

Name: Agapito Martinez
District Court: County Court, County of Webb, Laredo, Texas   **Address:** N.A.
Type of Record: Declaration of Intention, No. #1941
DOB: N.A. (36 years old) **Place:** Nuevo Laredo, Tamaulipas   **Last Foreign Residence:** N.A.
Married to: N.A.   **Date:** N.A.
Where: N.A.
Crossed the Border on: 1873
Where: Laredo, Texas   **Mode of travel:** N.A.
Date Certificate Issued: October 26, 1886
Alien Registration: N.A.
Description: N.A.

NATURALIZATION EXTRACTS

Name: Alberto Verdin Martinez
District Court: District Court, Ft. Scott, Kansas
Address: 1110 S. Steuben Ave. Chanute, Neosho County, Kansas **Type of Record:** Declaration of Intention
DOB: April 9, 1907 **Place:** Jesus Maria, Jalisco
Last Foreign Residence: Jesus Maria, Jalisco
Married to: Maria Martinez (nee Baldivio) **Date:** July 7, 1931 **Where:** Erie, Kansas (Maria was born at Las Trojas, Mexico, on Oct. 17, 1895. She entered the U.S. at El Paso, Texas, on June 22, 1912.)
Crossed the Border on: June 12, 1920 (Crossed the border under the name of Alberto Martinez) **Where:** Laredo, Texas **Mode of travel:** International Bridge **Date Certificate Issued:** July 19, 1938
Alien Registration: N.A.
Description: Occupation: Laborer. Light Tan Complexion, Brown Eyes, Black Hair, 5 Feet, 1½ Inches, 122 Pounds. Six children listed – all born between 1927 and 1938.

NATURALIZATION EXTRACTS

Name: Carmen Martinez
District Court: District Court, Los Angeles, California
Address: 6604 S. Hoover Ave., Los Angeles, California
Type of Record: Petition for Naturalization, No. 70898 (695990)   **DOB:** May 24, 1917 **Place:** Zacatecas, Mexico
Last Foreign Residence: Juarez, Chihuahua
Married to: Not married **Date:** N.A.
Where: N.A.
Crossed the Border on: June 17, 1922
Where: El Paso, Texas **Mode of travel:** El Paso Electric Railway (Certificate of Arrival, No. 23-51896)
Date Certificate Issued: January 4, 1940 (Declaration of Intention No. 79616 (No. 58016) filed on Jan. 2, 1937 in District Court, Los Angeles, California)
Alien Registration: N.A.
Description: Occupation: Student. Race: Syrian. Light Complexion, Brown Eyes, Brown Hair, 5 Feet, 0 Inches, 125 Pounds..

NATURALIZATION EXTRACTS

Name: Francisco Martinez

District Court: County Court, County of Maverick, Eagle Pass, Texas

Address: N.A.

Type of Record: Declaration of Intention

DOB: N.A.   **Place:** Lampazos, Nuevo Leon

Last Foreign Residence: N.A.

Married to: N.A.   **Date:** N.A.

Where: N.A.

Crossed the Border on: April 1883

Where: Laredo, Texas   **Mode of travel:** N.A.

Date Certificate Issued: November 3, 1884

Alien Registration: N.A.

Description: N.A.

NATURALIZATION EXTRACTS

Name: Manuel Martinez
District Court: District Court, Los Angeles, California
Address: 341 First St., San Pedro, California
Type of Record: Petition for Naturalization, No. 70868 (695877) **DOB:** Feb. 27, 1905 **Place:** Chihuahua, Mexico
Last Foreign Residence: Chihuahua, Mexico
Married to: Maria **Date:** June 10, 1932
Where: Los Angeles, California (Maria was born at Douglas, Arizona, on June 10, 1910.) **Crossed the Border on:** May 20, 1915
Where: El Paso, Texas **Mode of travel:** Streetcar (Certificate of Arrival, No. 23-45487) **Date Certificate Issued:** January 4, 1940 (Declaration of Intention No. 75234 filed on April 10, 1936 in District Court, Los Angeles, California) **Alien Registration:** N.A.
Description: Occupation: Stevedore. Three children listed – all born between 1933 and 1938.

NATURALIZATION EXTRACTS

Name: Manuel Verdin Martinez
District Court: District Court, Ft. Scott, Kansas
Address: 1125 S. Steuben Ave. Chanute, Neosho County, Kansas **Type of Record:** Declaration of Intention
DOB: April 21, 1908 **Place:** Jesus Maria, Jalisco
Last Foreign Residence: Jesus Maria, Jalisco
Married to: Maria Martinez (nee Leon) **Date:** February 2, 1935 **Where:** Lola, Kansas (Maria was born at Huanimaro, Guanajuato, on Oct. 5, 1912. She entered the U.S. at Laredo, Texas, on May 17, 1916.) **Crossed the Border on:** June 12, 1920 (Crossed the border under the name of Manuel Verdin Martinez) **Where:** Laredo, Texas **Mode of travel:** Train (Certificate of Arrival, No. 16-3427) **Date Certificate Issued:** February 15, 1939
Alien Registration: N.A.
Description: Occupation: Laborer. Light Tan Complexion, Brown Eyes, Black Hair, 5 Feet, 2 Inches, 120 Pounds. Three children listed – all born between 1935 and 1938.

NATURALIZATION EXTRACTS

Name: Ygnacio Martinez
District Court: County Court, County of Webb, Laredo, Texas **Address:** N.A.
Type of Record: Declaration of Intention, No. #1989
DOB: N.A. (39 years old) **Place:** San Carlos Cunda, Mexico **Last Foreign Residence:** N.A.
Married to: N.A.   **Date:** N.A.
Where: N.A.
Crossed the Border on: June 30, 1867
Where: Eagle Pass, Texas **Mode of travel:** N.A.
Date Certificate Issued: October 30, 1886
Alien Registration: N.A.
Description: N.A.

NATURALIZATION EXTRACTS

Name: Dolores Martini
District Court: District Court, Los Angeles, California
Address: 4254 2nd Ave., Los Angeles, California
Type of Record: Petition for Naturalization, No. 68591 (No. 472198)   **DOB:** April 15, 1903 **Place:** Guadalajara, Jalisco
Last Foreign Residence: Mexico City, Mexico
Married to: Alipio Martini **Date:** May 12, 1930
Where: Los Angeles, California (Alipio was born at Serra de Conti, Italy, on Feb. 22, 1888. He entered the U.S. at New York on Oct. 10, 1910.)
Crossed the Border on: Sept. 3, 1928 (Crossed under the name of Dolores Guzman Vargas de Chretinneau)   **Where:** El Paso, Texas **Mode of travel:** EN de M Railroad (Certificate of Arrival, No. 23-71305)   **Date Certificate Issued:** October 4, 1939
Alien Registration: N.A.
Description: Occupation: Housewife. Husband was a citizen of the U.S. by naturalization in U.S. District Court at Los Angeles, California, on March 10, 1933.

NATURALIZATION EXTRACTS

Name: Antonio Ladislao Maza aka Tony Maza
District Court: Superior Court, Cochise County, State of Arizona **Address:** 706 Eighth Street, Douglas, Arizona
Type of Record: Declaration of Intention, No. 997 (328699) **DOB:** June 13, 1895   **Place:** Laredo, Mexico
Last Foreign Residence: Naco, Sonora
Married to: Not married   **Date:** N.A.
Where: N.A.
Crossed the Border on: 1899
Where: Laredo, Texas   **Mode of travel:** Walked across **Date Certificate Issued:** May 7, 1917
Alien Registration: N.A.
Description: Occupation: Clerk. Dark Complexion, 5 Feet, 8 Inches, 145 Pounds, Brown Hair, Brown Eyes.

NATURALIZATION EXTRACTS

Name: Esteban Mendes
District Court: County Court, County of Webb, Laredo, Texas **Address:** N.A.
Type of Record: Declaration of Intention, No. #1918
DOB: N.A. (38 years old) **Place:** Saltillo, Coahuila
Last Foreign Residence: N.A.
Married to: N.A.   **Date:** N.A.
Where: N.A.
Crossed the Border on: August 5, 1884
Where: Palafox, Texas **Mode of travel:** N.A.
Date Certificate Issued: October 29, 1886
Alien Registration: N.A.
Description: N.A.

NATURALIZATION EXTRACTS

Name: Jose M. Mendiola
District Court: County Court, County of Webb, Laredo, Texas   **Address:** N.A.
Type of Record: Declaration of Intention
DOB: N.A. (23 years old) **Place:** Vallecillo, Nuevo Leon
Last Foreign Residence: N.A.
Married to: N.A. **Date:** N.A.
Where: N.A.
Crossed the Border on: 1880
Where: Laredo, Texas **Mode of travel:** N.A.
Date Certificate Issued: November 7, 1892
Alien Registration: N.A.
Description: N.A.

NATURALIZATION EXTRACTS

Name: Andres Mendoza
District Court: Superior Court, Cochise County, State of Arizona **Address:** Guaymas, Sonora
Type of Record: Declaration of Intention, No. 97856
DOB: Nov. 30, 1892   **Place:** Guaymas, Sonora
Last Foreign Residence: Cananea, Sonora
Married to: N.A.   **Date:** N.A.
Where: N.A.
Crossed the Border on: May 20, 1906
Where: Naco, Arizona   **Mode of travel:** C.R.Y.V.P. Railroad **Date Certificate Issued:** December 9, 1914
Alien Registration: N.A.
Description: Occupation: Laborer. Dark Complexion, 6 Feet, 0 Inches, 152 Pounds, Black Hair, Brown Eyes.

NATURALIZATION EXTRACTS

Name: Pedro Mendoza
District Court: District Court, Topeka, Kansas
Address: 215 N. Chandler, Topeka, Kansas
Type of Record: Petition for Naturalization
DOB: Dec. 2, 1894 **Place:** Silao, Guanajuato
Last Foreign Residence: N.A.
Married to: Evelyn Stager Mendoza **Date:** May 13, 1928
Where: Topeka, Kansas (Evelyn was born at Lawrence, Kansas, on August 7, 1904.)   **Crossed the Border on:** June 18, 1913
Where: El Paso, Texas **Mode of travel:** El Paso Electric Railway   **Date Certificate Issued:** N.A.
Alien Registration: N.A.
Description: Occupation: Laborer. Dark Complexion, 5 Feet, 5 Inches, 154 Pounds, Brown Hair, Brown Eyes. Four children listed – all born between 1929 and 1936.

NATURALIZATION EXTRACTS

Name: Eutemio Mesa
District Court: Superior Court, Cochise County, State of Arizona   **Address:** 16th Street, Douglas, Arizona
Type of Record: Declaration of Intention, No. 947 (328649)   **DOB:** Dec. 24, 1878   **Place:** Alamos, Sonora
Last Foreign Residence: Alamos, Sonora
Married to: N.A.   **Date:** N.A.
Where: N.A.
Crossed the Border on: June 8, 1904
Where: Naco, Arizona   **Mode of travel:** Sud-Pacifico de Mexico Railroad   **Date Certificate Issued:** December 23, 1916
Alien Registration: N.A.
Description: Occupation: Brick Mason. Dark Complexion, 5 Feet, 10 Inches, 155 Pounds, Black Hair, Brown Eyes.

NATURALIZATION EXTRACTS

Name: Guillermo Miesti
District Court: County Court, County of Webb, Laredo, Texas   **Address:** N.A.
Type of Record: Declaration of Intention
DOB: N.A. (63 years old) **Place:** Salinas Victoria, Nuevo Leon   **Last Foreign Residence:** N.A.
Married to: N.A.   **Date:** N.A.
Where: N.A.
Crossed the Border on: December 15, 1892
Where: Laredo, Texas   **Mode of travel:** N.A.
Date Certificate Issued: November 5, 1892
Alien Registration: N.A.
Description: N.A.

NATURALIZATION EXTRACTS

Name: Maria Barrientos Moncada

District Court: District Court, Los Angeles, California

Address: 1711 Brooklyn Ave., Los Angeles, California

Type of Record: Petition for Naturalization, No. 71113 (696285)
DOB: Sept. 10, 1901 **Place:** Torreon, Coahuila

Last Foreign Residence: Torreon, Coahuila

Married to: Jose Leon Moncada **Date:** Dec. 24, 1919

Where: Eastland, Texas (Jose was born at Santa Barbara, Chihuahua, on May 8, 1892. He entered the U.S. on Feb. 20, 1911.)
Crossed the Border on: October 10, 1916

Where: El Paso, Texas **Mode of travel:** Street car

Date Certificate Issued: January 15, 1940

Alien Registration: N.A.
Description: Occupation: Maid. Seven children listed – all born between 1922 and 1934. Husband Jose Leon Moncada was naturalized on May 25, 1934, at U.S. District Court in Los Angeles, California (Certificate 3839094).

NATURALIZATION EXTRACTS

Name: Gregorio Morales
District Court: County Court, County of Maverick, Eagle Pass, Texas **Address:** N.A.
Type of Record: Declaration of Intention
DOB: N.A. (30 years old) **Place:** Monclova, Coahuila
Last Foreign Residence: N.A.
Married to: N.A.   **Date:** N.A.
Where: N.A.
Crossed the Border on: August 1883
Where: Eagle Pass, Texas **Mode of travel:** N.A.
Date Certificate Issued: November 1, 1884
Alien Registration: N.A.
Description: N.A.

NATURALIZATION EXTRACTS

Name: Victor Morales
District Court: County Court, County of Webb, Laredo, Texas
Address: N.A.
Type of Record: Declaration of Intention
DOB: N.A. (27 years old) **Place:** Candela, Coahuila
Last Foreign Residence: N.A.
Married to: N.A.   **Date:** N.A.
Where: N.A.
Crossed the Border on: January 15, 1904
Where: Laredo, Texas **Mode of travel:** N.A.
Date Certificate Issued: January 29, 1906
Alien Registration: N.A.
Description: N.A.

NATURALIZATION EXTRACTS

Name: Antonio Morin
District Court: County Court, County of Webb, Laredo, Texas **Address:** N.A.
Type of Record: Declaration of Intention, No. #2023
DOB: N.A. (33 years old) **Place:** Monterrey, Nuevo Leon
Last Foreign Residence: N.A.
Married to: N.A.   **Date:** N.A.
Where: N.A.
Crossed the Border on: April 10, 1878
Where: Brownsville, Texas **Mode of travel:** N.A.
Date Certificate Issued: November 1, 1886
Alien Registration: N.A.
Description: N.A.

NATURALIZATION EXTRACTS

Name: Francisco Munoz
District Court: District Court, Topeka, Kansas
Address: 315 Branner St., Topeka, Kansas
Type of Record: Petition for Naturalization, No. 514908
DOB: April 22, 1904   **Place:** Leon, Guanajuato
Last Foreign Residence: Guadalajara, Jalisco
Married to: Mary T. Munoz   **Date:** March 24, 1927
Where: Topeka, Kansas (Mary was born in Spencer, Kansas, on June 22, 1912.)   **Crossed the Border on:** September 12, 1923
Where: Laredo, Texas   **Mode of travel:** Footbridge (Certificate of Arrival, No. 16-3967)   **Date Certificate Issued:** December 28, 1939
Alien Registration: N.A.
Description: Occupation: Motor Truck Operator. Six children listed – all born between 1928 and 1939.

NATURALIZATION EXTRACTS

Name: Antonio Nabarrete
District Court: District Court, Southern District of California, Los Angeles, California   **Address:** 1256 S. Main, Pomona, Los Angeles County, California   **Type of Record:** Declaration of Intention
DOB: Dec. 19, 1908 **Place:** Penjamo, Guanajuato
Last Foreign Residence: Penjamo, Guanajuato
Married to: Maria **Date:** November 8, 1935
Where: Salinas, California (Maria was born in Guanacevi, Durango, on May 12, 1905. She entered the U.S. at San Ysidro, California, on Aug. 29, 1941.)   **Crossed the Border on:** February 25, 1913
Where: El Paso, Texas **Mode of travel:** Street car (Certificate of Arrival, No. 23R133090)   **Date Certificate Issued:** July 18, 1945
Alien Registration: N.A.
Description: Occupation: Molder. Dark Complexion, 5 Feet, 6½ Inches, Brown Eyes, Black Hair, 180 Pounds. One child listed – born in 1936.

NATURALIZATION EXTRACTS

Name: Maria Ayala Nabarrete
District Court: District Court, Southern District of California, Los Angeles, California   **Address:** 1256 S. Main, Pomona, Los Angeles County, California   **Type of Record:** Declaration of Intention
DOB: May 12, 1905 **Place:** Guanacevi, Durango
Last Foreign Residence: Tijuana, Baja California
Married to: Antonio **Date:** November 8, 1935
Where: Salinas, California (Antonio was born in Penjamo, Guanajuato, on Dec. 19, 1908. He entered the U.S. at El Paso, Texas, on Feb. 25, 1913.)
Crossed the Border on: August 29, 1941 (Crossed under the name of Maria Ayala de Nabarrete)   **Where:** San Ysidro, California **Mode of travel:** Foot (Certificate of Arrival, No. 23-133091)   **Date Certificate Issued:** July 18, 1945
Alien Registration: N.A.
Description: Occupation: Housewife. Dark Complexion, 4 Feet, 8 Inches, Dark Brown Eyes, Black Hair, 85 Pounds. One child listed – born in 1936.

NATURALIZATION EXTRACTS

Name: Francis Nava
District Court: District Court, District of Colorado, Denver, Colorado **Address:** 1300 South Steele Street, Denver, Colorado
Type of Record: Declaration of Intention
DOB: Jan. 16,1915   **Place:** Purisima del Rincon, Guanajuato **Last Foreign Residence:** Purisima del Rincon, Guanajuato
Married to: Not married   **Date:** N.A.
Where: N.A.
Crossed the Border on: Dec. 11, 1916 (Crossed under the name of Francisco Nava) **Where:** El Paso, Texas   **Mode of travel:** El Paso Electric Railway (Certificate of Arrival, No. 18-13523) **Date Certificate Issued:** January 19, 1944
Alien Registration: N.A.
Description: Occupation: Divinity Student. Dark complexion, 5 Feet, 7½ Inches, 135 Pounds, Black Hair, Brown Eyes.

NATURALIZATION EXTRACTS

Name: Gregorio Nuños
District Court: County Court, County of Maverick, Eagle Pass, Texas **Address:** N.A.
Type of Record: Declaration of Intention
DOB: N.A. (70 years old) **Place:** Real de Sombrerete, Zacatecas **Last Foreign Residence:** N.A.
Married to: N.A. **Date:** N.A.
Where: N.A.
Crossed the Border on: February 1888
Where: Eagle Pass, Texas **Mode of travel:** N.A.
Date Certificate Issued: November 7, 1892
Alien Registration: N.A.
Description: N.A.

NATURALIZATION EXTRACTS

Name: Jesus Leon Ojeda
District Court: Superior Court, Cochise County, State of Arizona **Address:** Box 2194, Bisbee, Arizona
Type of Record: Declaration of Intention, No. 407 (57855)
DOB: Feb. 24, 1879 **Place:** San Jose, Mexico
Last Foreign Residence: Cananea, Sonora
Married to: N.A. **Date:** N.A.
Where: N.A.
Crossed the Border on: November 24, 1905
Where: Naco, Arizona **Mode of travel:** Cananea Rio Yaqui and Pacific Railroad **Date Certificate Issued:** Sept. 16, 1914
Alien Registration: N.A.
Description: Occupation: Miner. Dark Complexion, 5 Feet, 10 Inches, 145 Pounds, Black Hair, Brown Eyes.

NATURALIZATION EXTRACTS

Name: Ynocente Olivares
District Court: County Court, County of Webb, Laredo, Texas   **Address:** N.A.
Type of Record: Declaration of Intention
DOB: N.A. (45 years old) **Place:** Lampazos, Nuevo Leon
Last Foreign Residence: N.A.
Married to: N.A.   **Date:** N.A.
Where: N.A.
Crossed the Border on: March 24, 1886
Where: Laredo, Texas   **Mode of travel:** N.A.
Date Certificate Issued: January 27, 1906
Alien Registration: N.A.
Description: N.A.

NATURALIZATION EXTRACTS

Name: Elena Ornelas
District Court: District Court, Southern District of California, Los Angeles, California **Address:** 111 N. Ditman Ave., Los Angeles, California
Type of Record: Declaration of Intention, No. 125810
DOB: Aug. 18, 1890   **Place:** Cuiteco, Chihuahua
Last Foreign Residence: Guadalajara, Jalisco
Married to: Efren   **Date:** April 12, 1912
Where: Cuiteco, Chihuahua (Efren was born in Guadalajara, Jalisco, on Sept, 21, 1884. He entered the U.S. at San Ysidro, California, on Dec. 20, 1945.)
Crossed the Border on: Dec. 20, 1945 (Crossed under the name of Elena Loya de Ornelas) **Where:** San Ysidro, California   **Mode of travel:** Foot (Certificate of Arrival, No. 1600-X-2076) **Date Certificate Issued:** May 1, 1946
Alien Registration: N.A.
Description: Occupation: Housewife. Fair Complexion, 5 Feet, 6 Inches, 165 Pounds, Brown Eyes, Brown Hair.

NATURALIZATION EXTRACTS

Name: Ventura Ornelas
District Court: District Court, Ft. Scott, Kansas
Address: 1110 S. Steuben Ave. Chanute, Neosho County, Kansas   **Type of Record:** Declaration of Intention
DOB: July 14, 1898   **Place:** Ocotlan, Jalisco
Last Foreign Residence: Jamay, Jalisco
Married to: Tibursia   **Date:** May 28, 1928   **Where:** Erie, Kansas (Tibursia was born at Aguascalientes, Aguascalientes, on April 14, 1916. She entered the U.S. at Laredo, Texas, on June 10, 1920.)   **Crossed the Border on:** February 18, 1919
Where: Laredo, Texas   **Mode of travel:** Footbridge (Certificate of Arrival, No. 16-7114)   **Date Certificate Issued:** August 9, 1940
Alien Registration: N.A.
Description: Occupation: Unemployed Laborer. Three children listed – all born between 1930 and 1934.

NATURALIZATION EXTRACTS

Name: Manuel Ma. Orosco
District Court: County Court, County of Webb, Laredo, Texas **Address:** N.A.
Type of Record: Declaration of Intention
DOB: N.A. (22 years old) **Place:** Matamoros, Tamaulipas
Last Foreign Residence: N.A.
Married to: N.A.   **Date:** N.A.
Where: N.A.
Crossed the Border on: June 23, 1882
Where: Brownsville, Texas **Mode of travel:** N.A.
Date Certificate Issued: November 22, 1886
Alien Registration: N.A.
Description: N.A.

NATURALIZATION EXTRACTS

Name: Cayetano Eusclio Ortega
District Court: Superior Court, Cochise County, State of Arizona **Address:** Douglas, Arizona
Type of Record: Declaration of Intention, No. 808 (107315) **DOB:** Aug. 4, 1886 **Place:** Colonia Morelos, Mexico
Last Foreign Residence: Colonia Morelos, Mexico
Married to: N.A. **Date:** N.A.
Where: N.A.
Crossed the Border on: May 19, 1915
Where: Douglas, Arizona **Mode of travel:** By wagon and team **Date Certificate Issued:** November 22, 1915
Alien Registration: N.A.
Description: Occupation: Farmer. Dark Complexion, 5 Feet, 7 Inches, 153 Pounds, Black Hair, Brown Eyes.

NATURALIZATION EXTRACTS

Name: Raymond Clyde Ortega
District Court: District Court, Topeka, Kansas
Address: 1323 E. Polk St., Topeka, Kansas
Type of Record: Petition for Naturalization
DOB: Oct. 31, 1910 **Place:** Santa Catarina Tepehuanes, Durango **Last Foreign Residence:** Santa Catarina Tepehuanes, Durango **Married to:** Virginia Munos **Date:** March 30, 1940
Where: Topeka, Kansas (Virginia was born in Willard, Kansas, on May 21, 1919.) **Crossed the Border on:** August 29, 1911
Where: El Paso, Texas **Mode of travel:** El Paso Electric Railway (Certificate of Arrival, No. 16-15045) **Date Certificate Issued:** January 23, 1942
Alien Registration: N.A.
Description: Occupation: Laborer. Dark Complexion, 5 Feet, 5 Inches, Brown Eyes, Black Hair. Two children listed – born in 1941 and 1942.

NATURALIZATION EXTRACTS

Name: Samuel Ortiz
District Court: District Court, Los Angeles, California
Address: 10620 Graham Ave., Los Angeles, California
Type of Record: Petition for Naturalization, No. 70910
DOB: Jan. 12, 1912 **Place:** Monterrey, Nuevo Leon
Last Foreign Residence: Monterrey, Nuevo Leon
Married to: Not married   **Date:** N.A.
Where: N.A.
Crossed the Border on: April 28, 1912
Where: Laredo, Texas **Mode of travel:** National Railways of Mexico (Certificate of Arrival, No. 23-27370)
Date Certificate Issued: January 5, 1940 (Declaration of Intention 63343 (No. 71111) filed on July 19, 1933 in District Court, Los Angeles, California)
Alien Registration: N.A.
Description: Occupation: Sheet metal worker. Dark Complexion, Brown Eyes, Black Hair, 5 Feet, 10 Inches, 159 Pounds.

NATURALIZATION EXTRACTS

Name: Benjamin Pacheco

District Court: District Court, Southern District of California, Los Angeles, California
Address: 3765 E. Dozier St., Los Angeles, California

Type of Record: Declaration of Intention, No. 125768

DOB: March 31, 1909 **Place:** Zacatecas, Zacatecas

Last Foreign Residence: Chihuahua, Chihuahua

Married to: Helen **Date:** April 26, 1942

Where: Los Angeles, California (Helen was born in Guadalajara, Jalisco, on Feb. 23, 1918. She entered the U.S. at El Paso, Texas, on 1924.)
Crossed the Border on: February 4, 1914

Where: El Paso, Texas **Mode of travel:** Foot (Certificate of Arrival, No. 23-111803)
Date Certificate Issued: April 23, 1946

Alien Registration: N.A.

Description: Occupation: Laborer. Dark Complexion, 5 Feet, 6½ Inch, 128 Pounds, Black Hair, Brown Eyes. One child listed – born in 1945.

NATURALIZATION EXTRACTS

Name: Esteban Padron
District Court: County Court, County of Webb, Laredo, Texas   **Address:** N.A.
Type of Record: Declaration of Intention
DOB: N.A. (24 years old) **Place:** Matamoros, Tamaulipas
Last Foreign Residence: N.A.
Married to: N.A.   **Date:** N.A.
Where: N.A.
Crossed the Border on: June 19, 1890
Where: Edinburgh, Texas **Mode of travel:** N.A.
Date Certificate Issued: November 5, 1892
Alien Registration: N.A.
Description: N.A.

NATURALIZATION EXTRACTS

Name: Juan B. Palma
District Court: District Court, District of Colorado, Denver, Colorado **Address:** 1552 Clay Street, Denver, Colorado
Type of Record: Declaration of Intention, No. 13131 (13482) **DOB:** May 4, 1899   **Place:** Atotonilco, El Alto, Jalisco
Last Foreign Residence: Atotonilco, El Alto, Jalisco
Married to: Dolores Soberanes   **Date:** Aug. 1, 1923
Where: Denver, Colorado (Dolores was born in Cuerna Baca, Mexico [Cuernavaca, Morelos ?] on Oct. 21, 1899. She entered the U.S. in January 1911 at El Paso, Texas.)
Crossed the Border on: August 23, 1938 (Crossed under the name of Juan Billalovos Palma)
Where: Laredo, Texas   **Mode of travel:** Raft (Certificate of Arrival, No. 18-8553)
Date Certificate Issued: August 23, 1938
Alien Registration: N.A.
Description: Occupation: Laborer. Dark complexion, 5 Feet, 5 Inches, 143 Pounds, Black Hair, Brown Eyes.

NATURALIZATION EXTRACTS

Name: Juan Pantoja aka John Pantoja
District Court: District Court, District of Colorado, Denver, Colorado **Address:** 1843 W. Myrtle Place, Denver, Colorado
Type of Record: Declaration of Intention, No. 12458 (17192) **DOB:** Dec. 2, 1890 **Place:** Uriangato, Mexico
Last Foreign Residence: Maro Leon, Guanajuato
Married to: Maria L. Pantoja **Date:** Nov. 22, 1922
Where: Denver, Colorado (Maria was born in Walsenburg, Colorado on August 10, 1887.) **Crossed the Border on:** January 26, 1927 (Crossed under the name of Juan Pantoja) **Where:** Laredo, Texas **Mode of travel:** Footbridge (Certificate of Arrival, No. 18-9042) **Date Certificate Issued:** July 18, 1936
Alien Registration: N.A.
Description: Occupation: Laborer. Dark complexion, 5 Feet, 4 Inches, 145 Pounds, Black Hair, Blue-gray Eyes. One child listed – born in 1921.

NATURALIZATION EXTRACTS

Name: Jose Barragan Parra
District Court: District Court, Southern District of California, Los Angeles, California   **Address:** 143½ E. 49th St., Los Angeles, California
Type of Record: Declaration of Intention, No. 106603
DOB: March 19, 1884 **Place:** Sonoyta, Sonora
Last Foreign Residence: N.A.
Married to: Rita   **Date:** October 19, 1906
Where: Superior, Arizona (Rita was born on Jan. 22, 1891 in Silverking, Arizona. Now deceased.)   **Crossed the Border on:** Obscured
Where: N.A.   **Mode of travel:** N.A.
Date Certificate Issued: April 26, 1941
Alien Registration: N.A.
Description: Occupation: Pipe Maker. Dark Complexion, 5 Feet, 8 Inches, 158 Pounds, Grey Hair, Brown Eyes. Ten children listed – all born between 1907 and 1931.

NATURALIZATION EXTRACTS

Name: Refugio Parra
District Court: District Court, District of Colorado, Denver, Colorado **Address:** 3288 South Acoma St., Englewood, Denver County, Colorado **Type of Record:** Declaration of Intention, No. 14666
DOB: June 22, 1909   **Place:** Aguascalientes, Mexico
Last Foreign Residence: Juarez, Chihuahua
Married to: Not married   **Date:** N.A.
Where: N.A.
Crossed the Border on: Sept. 14, 1917
Where: El Paso, Texas   **Mode of travel:** El Paso Electric Railway (Certificate of Arrival, No. 1103-K-1) **Date Certificate Issued:** March 11, 1946
Alien Registration: N.A.
Description: Occupation: Second Maid. Dark complexion, 4 Feet, 11 Inches, 105 Pounds, Black Hair, Brown Eyes.

NATURALIZATION EXTRACTS

Name: Dolores Patino
District Court: District Court, Southern District of California, Los Angeles, California **Address:** 1634 New Jersey St., Los Angeles, California
Type of Record: Declaration of Intention, No. 124113
DOB: Nov. 21, 1901   **Place:** Rosario, Sinaloa
Last Foreign Residence: Tijuana, Baja California
Married to: N.A.   **Date:** N.A.
Where: N.A.
Crossed the Border on: February 28, 1945 (Crossed under the name of Dolores Patino Vargara) **Where:** San Ysidro, California   **Mode of travel:** On foot (Certificate of Arrival, No. 23-104572) **Date Certificate Issued:** April 28, 1945
Alien Registration: N.A.
Description: Occupation: Seamstress. Medium Complexion, 5 Feet, 0 Inches, 110 Pounds, Brown Hair, Brown Eyes.

NATURALIZATION EXTRACTS

Name: Daniel Gonzales Payan

District Court: District Court, Los Angeles, California

Address: 3611 E. 5th St., Los Angeles, California

Type of Record: Petition for Naturalization, No. 71201 (696258)
DOB: Dec. 23, 1902 **Place:** Chihuahua, Chihuahua

Last Foreign Residence: Chihuahua, Chihuahua

Married to: Inez   **Date:** December 30, 1930

Where: Los Angeles, California

Crossed the Border on: July 2, 1912 (Crossed under the name of Daniel Payan)
Where: El Paso, Texas   **Mode of travel:** El Paso Electric Railway (Certificate of Arrival, No. 23-73336)
Date Certificate Issued: January 20, 1940

Alien Registration: N.A.

Description: Occupation: Cook. One child listed – born in 1931.

NATURALIZATION EXTRACTS

Name: Agustin Pedraza

District Court: County Court, County of Maverick, Eagle Pass, Texas
Address: N.A.

Type of Record: Declaration of Intention

DOB: N.A. (28 years old) **Place:** San Luis Potosi, Mexico

Last Foreign Residence: N.A.

Married to: N.A.   **Date:** N.A.

Where: N.A.

Crossed the Border on: 1874

Where: Ringgold, Texas **Mode of travel:** N.A.

Date Certificate Issued: November 3, 1884

Alien Registration: N.A.

Description: N.A.

NATURALIZATION EXTRACTS

Name: Nasario Pedraza
District Court: County Court, County of Maverick, Eagle Pass, Texas **Address:** N.A.
Type of Record: Declaration of Intention
DOB: N.A. (27 years old) **Place:** Paso del Norte [now Ciudad Juarez], Chihuahua **Last Foreign Residence:** N.A.
Married to: N.A.   **Date:** N.A.
Where: N.A.
Crossed the Border on: 1860
Where: El Paso, Texas **Mode of travel:** N.A.
Date Certificate Issued: November 3, 1884
Alien Registration: N.A.
Description: N.A.

NATURALIZATION EXTRACTS

Name: Juan Perales
District Court: District Court, Southern District of California, Los Angeles, California   **Address:** 1526½ E. 1st St., Los Angeles, California
Type of Record: Declaration of Intention, No. 105333
DOB: Jan. 20, 1906   **Place:** Velardana, Durango
Last Foreign Residence: Juarez, Chihuahua
Married to: Not married   **Date:** N.A.
Where: N.A.
Crossed the Border on: May 21, 1925
Where: El Paso, Texas   **Mode of travel:** El Paso Electric Railway (Certificate of Arrival, No. 23-97671)   **Date Certificate Issued:** March 29, 1941
Alien Registration: N.A.
Description: Occupation: Laborer. Dark Complexion, Brown Eyes, Black Hair, 5 Feet, 6 Inches, 145 Pounds.

NATURALIZATION EXTRACTS

Name: Apolonio Perez
District Court: District Court, District of Colorado, Denver, Colorado **Address:** 2737 Lawrence St., Denver, Colorado
Type of Record: Declaration of Intention, No. 13787
DOB: Feb. 23, 1898   **Place:** Mexico City, Mexico
Last Foreign Residence: Mexico City, Mexico
Married to: Maria Perez   **Date:** Nov. 22, 1924
Where: Denver, Colorado (Maria was born on Feb. 7, 1901 at Chihuahua, Mexico. She entered the U.S. at El Paso, Texas, date unknown.) **Crossed the Border on:** September 15, 1915
Where: El Paso, Texas   **Mode of travel:** International Bridge (Certificate of Arrival, No. 19 R 11280) **Date Certificate Issued:** November 28, 1940
Alien Registration: N.A.
Description: Occupation: Foundry Work. Dark complexion, 5 Feet, 6 Inches, 155 Pounds, Black Hair, Brown Eyes. Seven children listed – all born between 1919 and 1938.

NATURALIZATION EXTRACTS

Name: Dolores Altamirano Perez
District Court: District Court, Southern District of California, Los Angeles, California **Address:** 3443 Lan Franco St., Los Angeles, California
Type of Record: Declaration of Intention, No. 125798
DOB: April 4, 1904   **Place:** Chihuahua, Mexico
Last Foreign Residence: Chihuahua, Mexico
Married to: Pedro   **Date:** May 14, 1943
Where: Camp Roberts, California (Pedro was born in Guanajuato, Mexico, on Dec. 16, 1909. He entered the U.S. at Calexico, California, on Nov. 16, 1917.) **Crossed the Border on:** May 4, 1921
Where: El Paso, Texas   **Mode of travel:** El Paso Electric Railroad (Certificate of Arrival, No. 1600-K-1661) **Date Certificate Issued:** April 29, 1946
Alien Registration: N.A.
Description: Occupation: Housewife. Dark Complexion, 5 Feet, 3 Inches, Brown Eyes, Black Hair, 117 Pounds. Three children listed – born in 1926 and 1931.

NATURALIZATION EXTRACTS

Name: Juan de la Cruz Perez

District Court: County Court, County of Maverick, Eagle Pass, Texas
Address: N.A.

Type of Record: Declaration of Intention

DOB: N.A. (25 years old) **Place:** San Pedro de Campo, Mexico
Last Foreign Residence: N.A.

Married to: N.A.   **Date:** N.A.

Where: N.A.

Crossed the Border on: 1892

Where: Laredo, Texas **Mode of travel:** N.A.

Date Certificate Issued: October 26, 1896

Alien Registration: N.A.

Description: N.A.

NATURALIZATION EXTRACTS

Name: Martin Perez
District Court: County Court, County of Webb, Laredo, Texas **Address:** N.A.
Type of Record: Declaration of Intention
DOB: N.A. (43 years old) **Place:** Doctor Arroyo, Nuevo Leon **Last Foreign Residence:** N.A.
Married to: N.A.   **Date:** N.A.
Where: N.A.
Crossed the Border on: May 1884
Where: Laredo, Texas   **Mode of travel:** N.A.
Date Certificate Issued: November 22, 1886
Alien Registration: N.A.
Description: N.A.

NATURALIZATION EXTRACTS

Name: Pedro Perez
District Court: County Court, County of Webb, Laredo, Texas
Address: N.A.
Type of Record: Declaration of Intention
DOB: N.A. (23 years old) **Place:** Doctor Arroyo, Nuevo Leon
Last Foreign Residence: N.A.
Married to: N.A.   **Date:** N.A.
Where: N.A.
Crossed the Border on: December 18, 1885
Where: Edinburgh, Texas   **Mode of travel:** N.A.
Date Certificate Issued: November 1, 1890
Alien Registration: N.A.
Description: N.A.

NATURALIZATION EXTRACTS

Name: Manuel Porras
District Court: County Court, County of Webb, Laredo, Texas   **Address:** N.A.
Type of Record: Declaration of Intention
DOB: N.A. (24 years old) **Place:** Nuevo Leon, Tamaulipas
Last Foreign Residence: N.A.
Married to: N.A.   **Date:** N.A.
Where: N.A.
Crossed the Border on: June 24, 1889
Where: Laredo, Texas **Mode of travel:** N.A.
Date Certificate Issued: November 5, 1892
Alien Registration: N.A.
Description: N.A.

NATURALIZATION EXTRACTS

Name: Juana Prieto aka Jane Ornelas Prieto
District Court: District Court, Southern District of California, Los Angeles, California **Address:** 1100 N. Garaghty Ave., Los Angeles, California
Type of Record: Declaration of Intention, No. 125757
DOB: June 1, 1922 **Place:** Namiquipa, Chihuahua
Last Foreign Residence: Namiquipa, Chihuahua
Married to: Edward Prieto   **Date:** July 25, 1942
Where: Artesia, California (Edward was born in Mexico City, Mexico, on July 15, 1915. He entered the U.S. at Douglas, Arizona, on April 30, 1916.)
Crossed the Border on: January 4, 1923 (Crossed under the name of Juana Ornelas)
Where: Columbus, New Mexico   **Mode of travel:** Automobile (Certificate of Arrival, No. 23-131931)
Date Certificate Issued: April 23, 1946
Alien Registration: N.A.
Description: Occupation: Housewife. Light Complexion, 5 Feet, 3 Inches, 112 Pounds, Brown Hair, Brown Eyes. Two children listed – born in 1943 and 1945.

NATURALIZATION EXTRACTS

Name: Antonio Ramirez
District Court: County Court, County of Maverick, Eagle Pass, Texas **Address:** N.A.
Type of Record: Declaration of Intention
DOB: N.A. (25 years old) **Place:** Aguadulce, Mexico
Last Foreign Residence: N.A.
Married to: N.A.   **Date:** N.A.
Where: N.A.
Crossed the Border on: December 15, 1891
Where: Eagle Pass, Texas   **Mode of travel:** N.A.
Date Certificate Issued: October 16, 1894
Alien Registration: N.A.
Description: N.A.

NATURALIZATION EXTRACTS

Name: John Ramirez
District Court: District Court, District of Colorado, Denver, Colorado **Address:** [Street name illegible], Denver, Colorado
Type of Record: Declaration of Intention, No. 12925 (17788) **DOB:** June 24, 1892   **Place:** San Juan, Jalisco
Last Foreign Residence: Piedras Negras, Coahuila
Married to: Not married (widowed)   **Date:** N.A.
Where: N.A.
Crossed the Border on: 1898
Where: Eagle Pass, Texas   **Mode of travel:** Railroad
Date Certificate Issued: November 22, 1937
Alien Registration: N.A.
Description: Occupation: Miner. Very dark complexion, 5 Feet, 4 Inches, 145 Pounds, Black Hair, Brown Eyes. Eight children listed – all born between 1912 and 1930.

NATURALIZATION EXTRACTS

Name: Pedro Garza Ramirez
District Court: County Court, County of Webb, Laredo, Texas   **Address:** N.A.
Type of Record: Declaration of Intention
DOB: N.A. (48 years old) **Place:** Guerrero, Tamaulipas
Last Foreign Residence: N.A.
Married to: N.A.   **Date:** N.A.
Where: N.A.
Crossed the Border on: September 20, 1889
Where: Carrizo, Texas   **Mode of travel:** N.A.
Date Certificate Issued: November 5, 1892
Alien Registration: N.A.
Description: N.A.

NATURALIZATION EXTRACTS

Name: Secundino Ramirez
District Court: County Court, County of Maverick, Eagle Pass, Texas **Address:** N.A.
Type of Record: Declaration of Intention
DOB: N.A. (32 years old) **Place:** Guadalajara, Jalisco
Last Foreign Residence: N.A.
Married to: N.A.   **Date:** N.A.
Where: N.A.
Crossed the Border on: September 1880
Where: Laredo, Texas **Mode of travel:** N.A.
Date Certificate Issued: October 16, 1894
Alien Registration: N.A.
Description: N.A.

NATURALIZATION EXTRACTS

Name: Basilio Ramos
District Court: District Court, Los Angeles, California
Address: 4235 E. 3rd St., Los Angeles, California
Type of Record: Petition for Naturalization, No. 70821 (No. 695887)
DOB: Feb. 23, 1892 **Place:** El Trunfo, Lower California [Baja California Sur] **Last Foreign Residence:** Cananea, Sonora
Married to: Maria Moroyoqui **Date:** April 2, 1919
Where: Cananea, Sonora (Maria was born at Mochicanui, Sinaloa, on Aug. 15, 1893. She entered the U.S. at Naco, Arizona, in June 1920.)
Crossed the Border on: June 11, 1923
Where: Naco, Arizona **Mode of travel:** Foot (Certificate of Arrival, No. 23-35901)
Date Certificate Issued: January 2, 1940 (Declaration of Intention 67690 (No. 12059) filed Nov. 19, 1934 in District Court, Los Angeles.)
Alien Registration: N.A.
Description: Occupation: Laborer. Light Complexion. Light Brown Eyes, Brown Hair, 5 Feet, 6 Inches, 200 Pounds. Five children listed – all born between 1920 and 1931.

NATURALIZATION EXTRACTS

Name: Cruz Rangel
District Court: County Court, County of Maverick, Eagle Pass, Texas
Address: N.A.
Type of Record: Declaration of Intention
DOB: N.A. (23 years old) **Place:** Ramos Arizpe, Coahuila
Last Foreign Residence: N.A.
Married to: N.A.   **Date:** N.A.
Where: N.A.
Crossed the Border on: September 16, 1891
Where: Eagle Pass, Texas   **Mode of travel:** N.A.
Date Certificate Issued: October 18, 1894
Alien Registration: N.A.
Description: N.A.

NATURALIZATION EXTRACTS

Name: Monico Rangel
District Court: Superior Court, Cochise County, State of Arizona **Address:** Willcox, Arizona
Type of Record: Declaration of Intention, No. 953 (328655) **DOB:** May 4, 1887　　**Place:** Yxuriguiqan, Mexico
Last Foreign Residence: Mexico City, Mexico
Married to: Not married　　　　**Date:** N.A.
Where: N.A.
Crossed the Border on: May 8, 1909
Where: El Paso, Texas　**Mode of travel:** Mexican Central Railroad **Date Certificate Issued:** January 27, 1917
Alien Registration: N.A.
Description: Occupation: Laborer. Dark Complexion, 5 Feet, 0 Inches, 115 Pounds, Dark Hair, Dark Eyes.

NATURALIZATION EXTRACTS

Name: Gonzalo Rascon
District Court: Superior Court, Cochise County, State of Arizona   **Address:** Sixth Street, Douglas, Arizona
Type of Record: Declaration of Intention, No. 1107 (276669)   **DOB:** 1892 **Place:** Moctezuma, Sonora
Last Foreign Residence: Moctezuma, Sonora
Married to: Not married (Wife dead) **Date:** N.A.
Where: N.A.
Crossed the Border on: 1906
Where: Douglas, Arizona **Mode of travel:** Nacozari Railway Train   **Date Certificate Issued:** September 22, 1917
Alien Registration: N.A.
Description: Occupation: Plumber. Dark Complexion, 5 Feet, 7 Inches, 150 Pounds, Black Hair, Black Eyes.

NATURALIZATION EXTRACTS

Name: Robert Garcia Redondo
District Court: Superior Court, Cochise County, State of Arizona **Address:** Box 979, Warren, Arizona
Type of Record: Declaration of Intention
DOB: Dec. 9, 1886   **Place:** Atlar, Sonora
Last Foreign Residence: Cananea, Sonora
Married to: N.A.   **Date:** N.A.
Where: N.A.
Crossed the Border on: December 22, 1907
Where: Naco, Arizona   **Mode of travel:** C.Y.R.P. Railroad **Date Certificate Issued:** Dec. 7, 1914
Alien Registration: N.A.
Description: Occupation: Assayer. Dark Complexion, 5 Feet, 8 ½ Inches, 140 Pounds, Black Hair, Brown Eyes.

NATURALIZATION EXTRACTS

Name: Alberto Renteria
District Court: District Court, Los Angeles, California
Address: 229 North Kern Ave., Los Angeles, California
Type of Record: Petition for Naturalization, No. 68943 (472442) **DOB:** Feb. 19, 1905   **Place:** Torreon, Coahuila
Last Foreign Residence: Torreon, Coahuila
Married to: Neva   **Date:** November 17, 1929
Where: Los Angeles, California (Neva was born in El Paso, Texas, on January 11, 1907.) **Crossed the Border on:** March 22, 1905
Where: El Paso, Texas   **Mode of travel:** N.A.
Date Certificate Issued: October 19, 1939
Alien Registration: N.A.
Description: Occupation: Laborer. One Child listed – born in 1930.

NATURALIZATION EXTRACTS

Name: Cruz Cosio Renteria
District Court: District Court, Topeka, Kansas
Address: 216 N. Branner, Topeka, Kansas
Type of Record: Petition for Naturalization, No. 403208
DOB: May 3, 1911   **Place:** Valparaiso, Zacatecas
Last Foreign Residence: Ciudad Juarez, Chihuahua
Married to: N.A.   **Date:** N.A.
Where: N.A.
Crossed the Border on: March 2, 1918 (Crossed under the name of Cruz Renteria y Cosio) **Where:** El Paso, Texas   **Mode of travel:** El Paso Electric Railway **Date Certificate Issued:** August 19, 1940
Alien Registration: N.A.
Description: Occupation: Butcher.

NATURALIZATION EXTRACTS

Name: Dionisio Reyes
District Court: District Court, District of Colorado, Denver, Colorado **Address:** Woponas, South Colorado
Type of Record: Declaration of Intention, No. 12605
DOB: March 5, 1887 **Place:** Parras, Coahuila
Last Foreign Residence: Monterrey, Nuevo Leon
Married to: Not married **Date:** N.A.
Where: N.A.
Crossed the Border on: January 1, 1914
Where: Laredo, Texas **Mode of travel:** Footbridge (Certificate of Arrival, No. 18-8967) **Date Certificate Issued:** November 27, 1936
Alien Registration: N.A.
Description: Occupation: Laborer. Dark Complexion, Brown Eyes, Black Hair, 5 Feet, 2½ Feet, 152 Pounds..

NATURALIZATION EXTRACTS

Name: Theodore Reyes
District Court: District Court, District of Colorado, Denver, Colorado **Address:** 1508 Dale Court, Denver, Colorado
Type of Record: Declaration of Intention, No. 14566 (21107) **DOB:** April 1, 1891 **Place:** Zacatecas, Zacatecas
Last Foreign Residence: Ciudad Juarez, Chihuahua
Married to: Eusebia Hernandez (separated) **Date:** 1923
Where: El Paso, Texas (Eusebia was born at Tampico, Mexico.) **Crossed the Border on:** July 13, 1926 (Crossed under the name of Teodore Reyes) **Where:** El Paso, Texas **Mode of travel:** El Paso Electric Railway (Certificate of Arrival, No. 19-17243) **Date Certificate Issued:** May 27, 1944
Alien Registration: N.A.
Description: Occupation: Music Teacher. Dark Complexion, 5 Feet, 4 Inches, 120 Pounds, Black-Gray Hair, Brown Eyes. Two children listed – born in 1924 and 1925.

NATURALIZATION EXTRACTS

Name: Pedro Reyna
District Court: Superior Court, Cochise County, State of Arizona **Address:** Fairbank, Arizona
Type of Record: Declaration of Intention, No. 701
DOB: June 29, 1860 **Place:** San Luis Potosi, Mexico
Last Foreign Residence: Santano, Mexico
Married to: N.A.　　　　　**Date:** N.A.
Where: N.A.
Crossed the Border on: November 6, 1906
Where: Nogales, Arizona　　**Mode of travel:** Sonora Railroad **Date Certificate Issued:** January 6, 1915
Alien Registration: N.A.
Description: Occupation: Laborer. Dark Complexion, 5 Feet, 6 Inches, 175 Pounds, Gray Hair, Brown Eyes.

NATURALIZATION EXTRACTS

Name: Enriqueta Rincon
District Court: District Court, Southern District of California, Los Angeles, California **Address:** 10112 Rosswoode Ave., South Gate, California
Type of Record: Declaration of Intention, No. 105248
DOB: August 4, 1905 **Place:** Guadalajara, Jalisco
Last Foreign Residence: Guadalajara, Jalisco
Married to: Manuel Rincon **Date:** Dec. 31, 1933
Where: Los Angeles, California (Manuel was born at Guadalajara, Jalisco, on Sept. 21, 1892. He entered the U.S. at El Paso, Texas, in November 1908.)
Crossed the Border on: February 16, 1923 (Crossed under the name of Enriqueta Zamarano)
Where: El Paso, Texas **Mode of travel:** El Paso Electric Railway (Certificate of Arrival, No. 23-89739)
Date Certificate Issued: March 28, 1941
Alien Registration: N.A.
Description: Occupation: Housewife. Medium Complexion, 5 Feet, 2 Inches, 130 Pounds, Dark Brown Hair, Brown Eyes. Three children listed – all born between 1934 and 1939.

NATURALIZATION EXTRACTS

Name: Jose Munoz Rivera
District Court: District Court, Los Angeles, California
Address: 10418 Fairgroves Ave., Tujunga, California
Type of Record: Petition for Naturalization, No. 71238 (696153)   **DOB:** Dec. 19, 1910   **Place:** Leon, Guanajuato
Last Foreign Residence: Leon, Guanajuato
Married to: Stella   **Date:** Dec. 16, 1933
Where: Los Angeles, California (Stella was born at Dulce, New Mexico, on January 22, 1914.)   **Crossed the Border on:** May 22, 1923 (Crossed under the name of Jose Rivera)   **Where:** El Paso, Texas   **Mode of travel:** El Paso Electric Railway (Certificate of Arrival, No. 23-74863)   **Date Certificate Issued:** January 22, 1940
Alien Registration: N.A.
Description: Occupation: Laborer. Two children listed – born in 1934 and 1937. Wife is a citizen by birth.

NATURALIZATION EXTRACTS

Name: Jesus Rocha

District Court: Superior Court, Cochise County, State of Arizona
Address: Bisbee, Arizona

Type of Record: Declaration of Intention, No. 725 (97567)

DOB: June 24, 1879   **Place:** Cananea, Sonora

Last Foreign Residence: Cananea, Sonora

Married to: N.A.   **Date:** N.A.

Where: N.A.

Crossed the Border on: May 8, 1907

Where: Naco, Arizona   **Mode of travel:** C.R.Y. & P. Railroad
Date Certificate Issued: December 19, 1914

Alien Registration: N.A.

Description: Occupation: Assayer. Dark Complexion, 5 Feet, 10 Inches, 160 Pounds, Black Hair, Brown Eyes.

NATURALIZATION EXTRACTS

Name: Refugio Gutierrez Rodarte
District Court: District Court, Southern District of California, Los Angeles, California   **Address:** 167 N. Herbert Ave., Los Angeles, California
Type of Record: Declaration of Intention, No. 125803
DOB: Jan. 18, 1894 **Place:** Parral, Chihuahua
Last Foreign Residence: Parral, Chihuahua
Married to: Atilano **Date:** July 13, 1913
Where: El Paso, Texas (Atilano was born in Plateros, Zacatecas, on Oct. 5, 1887. He entered the U.S. at El Paso, Texas, on April 27, 1907.)   **Crossed the Border on:** July 24, 1923 (Crossed under the name of Refugio Gutierrez)   **Where:** El Paso, Texas **Mode of travel:** El Paso Electric Railroad (Certificate of Arrival, No. 1600-K-2143)   **Date Certificate Issued:** April 30, 1946
Alien Registration: N.A.
Description: Occupation: Housewife. Medium Complexion, 5 Feet, 2½ Inches, Brown Eyes, Black Hair, 120 Pounds. Eight children listed – born in 1914 and 1931.

NATURALIZATION EXTRACTS

Name: Angel Rodrigues
District Court: County Court, County of Webb, Laredo, Texas
Address: N.A.
Type of Record: Declaration of Intention
DOB: N.A. (29 years old) **Place:** Zaragoza, Coahuila
Last Foreign Residence: N.A.
Married to: N.A.   **Date:** N.A.
Where: N.A.
Crossed the Border on: 1878
Where: Eagle Pass, Texas **Mode of travel:** N.A.
Date Certificate Issued: November 7, 1892
Alien Registration: N.A.
Description: N.A.

NATURALIZATION EXTRACTS

Name: Alvaro Rodriguez
District Court: District Court, Los Angeles, California
Address: 4435 Fisher St., Los Angeles, California
Type of Record: Petition for Naturalization, No. 68916 (474764)   **DOB:** Feb. 19, 1896 **Place:** Allende, Chihuahua
Last Foreign Residence: Ciudad Juarez, Chihuahua
Married to: Maria D. **Date:** July 17, 1916
Where: Los Angeles, California (Maria was born at Modlowa, Poland, on Jan. 2, 1893. She entered the U.S. at New York in 1910.)   **Crossed the Border on:** 1903
Where: El Paso, Texas **Mode of travel:** Wagon
Date Certificate Issued: October 17, 1939 (Declaration of Intention No. 78018 filed.)   **Alien Registration:** N.A.
Description: Occupation: Painter. Four children listed – all born between 1916 and 1922.

NATURALIZATION EXTRACTS

Name: Brigido Rodriguez
District Court: County Court, County of Webb, Laredo, Texas **Address:** N.A.
Type of Record: Declaration of Intention
DOB: N.A. (22 years old) **Place:** Guerrero, Tamaulipas
Last Foreign Residence: N.A.
Married to: N.A.　　　　**Date:** N.A.
Where: N.A.
Crossed the Border on: December 10, 1869
Where: Carrizo, Texas **Mode of travel:** N.A.
Date Certificate Issued: November 5, 1892
Alien Registration: N.A.
Description: N.A.

NATURALIZATION EXTRACTS

Name: David Genevivo Rodriguez
District Court: District Court, Southern District of California, Los Angeles, California **Address:** 825 N. Cordova St., Los Angeles, California
Type of Record: Declaration of Intention, No. 124171
DOB: Jan. 3, 1904 **Place:** Sauz, Guanajuato
Last Foreign Residence: Sauz, Guanajuato
Married to: Mary   **Date:** June 18, 1924
Where: Los Angeles, California (Mary was born on Aug. 15, 1900 in Mexico. She entered the U.S. at Calexico, California, in 1918.)
Crossed the Border on: July 29, 1936 (Crossed under the name of David G. Rodriguez)
Where: Calexico, California   **Mode of travel:** On foot (Certificate of Arrival, No. 23-132854)
Date Certificate Issued: May 7, 1945
Alien Registration: N.A.
Description: Occupation: Machinist. Dark Complexion, 5 Feet, 4 Inches, Dark Brown Eyes, Black Hair, 160 Pounds. Two children listed – born in 1935 and 1936.

NATURALIZATION EXTRACTS

Name: Jorge Rodriguez aka George Rodriguez
District Court: District Court, Southern District of California, Los Angeles, California **Address:** 813½ Centennial St., Los Angeles , California
Type of Record: Declaration of Intention
DOB: Oct. 20, 1923 **Place:** Guadalajara, Jalisco
Last Foreign Residence: Guadalajara, Jalisco
Married to: Not married   **Date:** N.A.
Where: N.A.
Crossed the Border on: November 21, 1927 (Crossed under the name of Jorge Ochoa) **Where:** Nogales, Arizona   **Mode of travel:** On foot (Certificate of Arrival, No. 23-133431) **Date Certificate Issued:** July 21, 1945
Alien Registration: N.A.
Description: Occupation: Freight Packager. Dark Complexion, 5 Feet, 4¾ Inches, Brown Eyes, Black Hair, 150 Pounds.

NATURALIZATION EXTRACTS

Name: Librado Rodriguez
District Court: County Court, County of Maverick, Eagle Pass, Texas **Address:** N.A.
Type of Record: Declaration of Intention
DOB: N.A. (24 years old)   **Place:** Piedras Negras, Coahuila **Last Foreign Residence:** N.A.
Married to: N.A.   **Date:** N.A.
Where: N.A.
Crossed the Border on: November 1865
Where: Eagle Pass, Texas   **Mode of travel:** N.A.
Date Certificate Issued: November 4, 1882
Alien Registration: N.A.
Description: N.A.

NATURALIZATION EXTRACTS

Name: Manuel Rodriguez
District Court: County Court, County of Webb, Laredo, Texas
Address: N.A.
Type of Record: Declaration of Intention
DOB: N.A. (26 years old) **Place:** Allende, Nuevo Leon
Last Foreign Residence: N.A.
Married to: N.A.   **Date:** N.A.
Where: N.A.
Crossed the Border on: December 15, 1869
Where: Carrizo, Texas **Mode of travel:** N.A.
Date Certificate Issued: November 5, 1892
Alien Registration: N.A.
Description: N.A.

NATURALIZATION EXTRACTS

Name: Tirso Rodriguez
District Court: County Court, County of Maverick, Eagle Pass, Texas **Address:** N.A.
Type of Record: Declaration of Intention
DOB: N.A. (23 years old)　　**Place:** Piedras Negras, Coahuila **Last Foreign Residence:** N.A.
Married to: N.A.　　**Date:** N.A.
Where: N.A.
Crossed the Border on: November 1874
Where: Eagle Pass, Texas　**Mode of travel:** N.A.
Date Certificate Issued: November 3, 1882
Alien Registration: N.A.
Description: N.A.

NATURALIZATION EXTRACTS

Name: Victoriano Rodriguez
District Court: County Court, County of Maverick, Eagle Pass, Texas   **Address:** N.A.
Type of Record: Declaration of Intention
DOB: N.A. (41 years old)　　**Place:** San Buenaventura, Mexico   **Last Foreign Residence:** N.A.
Married to: N.A.　　　　**Date:** N.A.
Where: N.A.
Crossed the Border on: 1872
Where: Eagle Pass, Texas　**Mode of travel:** N.A.
Date Certificate Issued: October 31, 1884
Alien Registration: N.A.
Description: N.A.

NATURALIZATION EXTRACTS

Name: Jose M.G. Rojas
District Court: County Court, County of Webb, Laredo, Texas   **Address:** N.A.
Type of Record: Declaration of Intention
DOB: N.A. (22 years old) **Place:** Nuevo Laredo, Tamaulipas   **Last Foreign Residence:** N.A.
Married to: N.A.   **Date:** N.A.
Where: N.A.
Crossed the Border on: December 20, 1898
Where: Laredo, Texas   **Mode of travel:** N.A.
Date Certificate Issued: January 22, 1906
Alien Registration: N.A.
Description: N.A.

NATURALIZATION EXTRACTS

Name: Consuelo Connie Romero
District Court: District Court, District of Colorado, Denver, Colorado **Address:** 2945 West 14th Avenue, Denver, Colorado
Type of Record: Declaration of Intention, No. 14582 (21186) **DOB:** March 21, 1922   **Place:** Chihuahua, Chihuahua
Last Foreign Residence: Chihuahua, Chihuahua
Married to: Not married   **Date:** N.A.
Where: N.A.
Crossed the Border on: July 12, 1922 (Crossed under the name of Consuelo Romero) **Where:** El Paso, Texas   **Mode of travel:** El Paso Electric Railway (Certificate of Arrival, No. 18-13864) **Date Certificate Issued:** August 14, 1944
Alien Registration: N.A.
Description: Occupation: Sales Clerk. Medium Dark complexion, 5 Feet, 0 Inches, 100 Pounds, Brown Hair, Brown Eyes.

NATURALIZATION EXTRACTS

Name: Luis Fernando Beaven Romero
District Court: District Court, Southern District of California, Los Angeles, California **Address:** 1120 Wilshire Blvd., Los Angeles, California
Type of Record: Declaration of Intention, No. 124186
DOB: Sept. 22, 1903　**Place:** Mexico City, Mexico
Last Foreign Residence: Cananea, Sonora
Married to: N.A.　**Date:** N.A.
Where: N.A.
Crossed the Border on: May 31, 1944
Where: Douglas, Arizona　**Mode of travel:** On foot (Certificate of Arrival, No. 23-132915) **Date Certificate Issued:** May 10, 1945
Alien Registration: N.A.
Description: Occupation: Civil Engineer. Dark Complexion, 5 Feet, 7 Inches, Brown Eyes, Black Hair, 170 Pounds.

NATURALIZATION EXTRACTS

Name: Pablo Romero
District Court: District Court, District of Colorado, Denver, Colorado **Address:** 1422 Canosa Court, Denver, Colorado
Type of Record: Declaration of Intention, No. 12884 (17734) **DOB:** Nov. 20, 1890   **Place:** Santamaria de Los Angeles, Mexico **Last Foreign Residence:** Chihuahua, Mexico
Married to: Felipa Romero   **Date:** April 15, 1911
Where: Chihuahua, Mexico (Felipa was born at Durango, Mexico, in 1897. She entered the U.S. at El Paso, Texas, on July 12, 1922.) **Crossed the Border on:** July 12, 1922
Where: El Paso, Texas   **Mode of travel:** El Paso Electric Railway (Certificate of Arrival, No. 18-10779) **Date Certificate Issued:** October 5, 1937
Alien Registration: N.A.
Description: Occupation: Laborer. Dark complexion, 5 Feet, 2 Inches, 120 Pounds, Black Hair, Brown Eyes. Twelve children listed – all born between 1912 and 1937.

NATURALIZATION EXTRACTS

Name: Refugio Romo
District Court: County Court, County of Maverick, Eagle Pass, Texas **Address:** N.A.
Type of Record: Declaration of Intention
DOB: N.A. (24 years old)   **Place:** Sacramento, Mexico
Last Foreign Residence: N.A.
Married to: N.A.   **Date:** N.A.
Where: N.A.
Crossed the Border on: 1879
Where: Eagle Pass, Texas   **Mode of travel:** N.A.
Date Certificate Issued: November 1, 1884
Alien Registration: N.A.
Description: N.A.

NATURALIZATION EXTRACTS

Name: Jesus Salinas
District Court: County Court, County of Maverick, Eagle Pass, Texas **Address:** N.A.
Type of Record: Declaration of Intention
DOB: N.A. (29 years old) **Place:** Monclova, Coahuila
Last Foreign Residence: N.A.
Married to: N.A. **Date:** N.A.
Where: N.A.
Crossed the Border on: July 17, 1882
Where: Eagle Pass, Texas **Mode of travel:** N.A.
Date Certificate Issued: October 19, 1886
Alien Registration: N.A.
Description: N.A.

NATURALIZATION EXTRACTS

Name: Santiago Salinas
District Court: County Court, County of Maverick, Eagle Pass, Texas   **Address:** N.A.
Type of Record: Declaration of Intention
DOB: N.A. (38 years old) **Place:** Matamoros, Tamaulipas   **Last Foreign Residence:** N.A.
Married to: N.A. **Date:** N.A.
Where: N.A.
Crossed the Border on: October 17, 1875
Where: Eagle Pass, Texas **Mode of travel:** N.A.
Date Certificate Issued: October 15, 1886
Alien Registration: N.A.
Description: N.A.

NATURALIZATION EXTRACTS

Name: Felipe Sanchez
District Court: County Court, County of Webb, Laredo, Texas **Address:** N.A.
Type of Record: Declaration of Intention, No. #1930
DOB: N.A. (22 years old) **Place:** Monclova, Coahuila
Last Foreign Residence: N.A.
Married to: N.A.   **Date:** N.A.
Where: N.A.
Crossed the Border on: May 5, 1880
Where: Brownsville, Texas **Mode of travel:** N.A.
Date Certificate Issued: October 27, 1886
Alien Registration: N.A.
Description: N.A.

NATURALIZATION EXTRACTS

Name: Manuel Sanchez
District Court: District Court, Los Angeles, California
Address: 747 E. 73rd St.., Los Angeles, California
Type of Record: Petition for Naturalization, No. 70993 (No. 695706)
DOB: Oct. 5, 1901 **Place:** San Juan de los Lagos, Jalisco
Last Foreign Residence: San Juan de los Lagos, Jalisco
Married to: Rosario   **Date:** April 3, 1921
Where: Los Angeles, California (Rosario was born at Guadalajara, Jalisco, on Aug. 14, 1904. She entered the U.S. at El Paso, Texas, on March 31, 1917.)
Crossed the Border on: August 10, 1911
Where: El Paso, Texas **Mode of travel:** El Paso Electric Railway (Certificate of Arrival, No. 23-51130)
Date Certificate Issued: January 9, 1940 (Declaration of Intention 79972 filed on Jan. 27, 1937 in District Court, Los Angeles, California)
Alien Registration: N.A.
Description: Occupation: Blacksmith

NATURALIZATION EXTRACTS

Name: Manuel Sanchez Sanchez
District Court: District Court, Southern District of California, Los Angeles, California **Address:** 753½ Lord St., Los Angeles, California
Type of Record: Declaration of Intention, No. 124086
DOB: Oct. 20, 1883   **Place:** Leon, Guanajuato
Last Foreign Residence: Villachuato, Mexcio
Married to: Not married   **Date:** N.A.
Where: N.A.
Crossed the Border on: June 23, 1909
Where: El Paso, Texas   **Mode of travel:** On foot (Certificate of Arrival, No. 23-118164) **Date Certificate Issued:** April 24, 1945
Alien Registration: N.A.
Description: Occupation: Laborer. Ruddy Complexion, Hazel Eyes, Black/Grey Hair, 5 Feet, 8 Feet, 158 Pounds..

NATURALIZATION EXTRACTS

Name: Felipe Sandoval	
District Court: County Court, County of Maverick, Eagle Pass, Texas	
Address: N.A.	
Type of Record: Declaration of Intention	
DOB: N.A. (48 years old)	**Place:** Monclova, Coahuila
Last Foreign Residence: N.A.	
Married to: N.A.	**Date:** N.A.
Where: N.A.	
Crossed the Border on: June 16, 1882	
Where: Eagle Pass, Texas	**Mode of travel:** N.A.
Date Certificate Issued: October 19, 1886	
Alien Registration: N.A.	
Description: N.A.	

NATURALIZATION EXTRACTS

Name: Benjamin Segura
District Court: District Court, Los Angeles, California
Address: 795 Clanton St., Los Angeles, California
Type of Record: Petition for Naturalization, No. 70941 (No. 691162)   **DOB:** Oct. 8, 1904 **Place:** Concepcion del Oro, Zacatecas
Last Foreign Residence: Concepcion del Oro, Zacatecas
Married to: Not married **Date:** N.A.
Where: N.A.
Crossed the Border on: November 14, 1929 (Crossed under the name of Benjamin Segura y Carrillo)   **Where:** El Paso, Texas **Mode of travel:** El Paso Electric Railway (Certificate of Arrival, No. 23-34152)   **Date Certificate Issued:** January 5, 1940 (Declaration of Intention 67294 (No. 36663) filed on Nov. 2, 1934 in District Court, Los Angeles, California)   **Alien Registration:** N.A.
Description: Occupation: Machinist. Dark Complexion, Dark Brown Eyes, Dark Brown Hair, 5 Feet, 7 Inches, 130 Pounds.

NATURALIZATION EXTRACTS

Name: Cesario Sepulveda
District Court: County Court, County of Webb, Laredo, Texas
Address: N.A.
Type of Record: Declaration of Intention
DOB: N.A. (79 years old) **Place:** Parras de la Fuente, Coahuila
Last Foreign Residence: N.A.
Married to: N.A.   **Date:** N.A.
Where: N.A.
Crossed the Border on: June 1897
Where: Laredo, Texas **Mode of travel:** N.A.
Date Certificate Issued: January 31, 1906
Alien Registration: N.A.
Description: N.A.

NATURALIZATION EXTRACTS

Name: Pedro Sepulveda
District Court: District Court, Los Angeles, California
Address: 1756 5th St., Santa Monica, California
Type of Record: Petition for Naturalization, No. 70838 (695750)
DOB: Oct. 23, 1889 **Place:** Hidalgo, Nuevo Leon
Last Foreign Residence: Cananea, Sonora
Married to: Teresa Avila **Date:** November 25, 1911
Where: Cananea, Sonora (Teresa was born at Guaymas, Sonora, on Oct. 15, 1896. She entered the U.S. at Naco, Arizona, on Nov. 18, 1913.)
Crossed the Border on: November 18, 1913
Where: Naco, Arizona **Mode of travel:** On foot (Certificate of Arrival, No. 23-40542)
Date Certificate Issued: January 2, 1940 (Declaration of Intention 76094 (No. 60494) filed on June 30, 1936 in District Court, Los Angeles, California)
Alien Registration: N.A.
Description: Occupation: Laborer. Dark Complexion, Brown Eyes, Black Hair, 5 Feet, 7 Inches, 124 Pounds. Eight children listed – all born between 1918 and 1933. Resided in Los Angeles County since March 1931.

NATURALIZATION EXTRACTS

Name: Narciso Serrano
District Court: District Court, Southern District of California, Los Angeles, California **Address:** 168 Alameda Ave., Azusa, Los Angeles County, California **Type of Record:** Declaration of Intention, No. 123827
DOB: Oct. 28, 1880   **Place:** Irapuato, Guanajuato
Last Foreign Residence: Irapuato, Guanajuato
Married to: Cumezinda   **Date:** Feb. 5, 1911
Where: Irapuato, Guanajuato (Cumezinda was born at Irapuato, Guanajuato, about Aug. 15, 1896. She entered the U.S. at El Paso, Texas, on July 27, 1923.) **Crossed the Border on:** May 4, 1922
Where: El Paso, Texas   **Mode of travel:** El Paso Electric Railroad (Certificate of Arrival, No. 23-111937) **Date Certificate Issued:** March 26, 1945
Alien Registration: N.A.
Description: Occupation: Laborer. Dark Complexion, 5 Feet, 5 Inches, Brown Eyes, Black Hair, 165 Pounds. Six children listed – all born between 1918 and 1931.

NATURALIZATION EXTRACTS

Name: Antonio Servantes
District Court: County Court, County of Webb, Laredo, Texas **Address:** N.A.
Type of Record: Declaration of Intention, No. #1943
DOB: N.A. (37 years old) **Place:** Monterrey, Nuevo Leon
Last Foreign Residence: N.A.
Married to: N.A.   **Date:** N.A.
Where: N.A.
Crossed the Border on: September 15, 1872
Where: Laredo, Texas **Mode of travel:** N.A.
Date Certificate Issued: October 26, 1886
Alien Registration: N.A.
Description: N.A.

NATURALIZATION EXTRACTS

Name: Lucas Sierra	
District Court: County Court, County of Maverick, Eagle Pass, Texas	
Address: N.A.	
Type of Record: Declaration of Intention	
DOB: N.A. (23 years old) **Place:** Parras, Coahuila	
Last Foreign Residence: N.A.	
Married to: N.A. **Date:** N.A.	
Where: N.A.	
Crossed the Border on: March 1883	
Where: Laredo, Texas **Mode of travel:** N.A.	
Date Certificate Issued: November 1, 1884	
Alien Registration: N.A.	
Description: N.A.	

NATURALIZATION EXTRACTS

Name: Concepcion Giron de Silva
District Court: District Court, Los Angeles, California
Address: 187 S. Eastern Ave., Los Angeles, California
Type of Record: Petition for Naturalization, No. 69071 (474841) **DOB:** May 8, 1900   **Place:** San Elizario, Texas
Last Foreign Residence: N.A.
Married to: Plutarco Silva   **Date:** March 17, 1922
Where: San Ygnacio, Mexico (Plutarco was born in San Ygnacio, Texas, on Dec. 21, 1896. He entered the U.S. at Isla, Texas, on April 20, 1910.) **Crossed the Border on:** N.A.
Where: N.A.   **Mode of travel:** N.A.
Date Certificate Issued: October 24, 1939 (Petition filed under Section 4, Act of 9/22/22, as amended.) **Alien Registration:** N.A.
Description: Occupation: Housewife. Seven children listed – born between 1918 and 1934.

NATURALIZATION EXTRACTS

Name: Jose Cornelio Solis
District Court: District Court, Topeka, Kansas
Address: 930 N. Topeka Ave., Topeka, Kansas
Type of Record: Petition for Naturalization
DOB: Sept. 16, 1908   **Place:** Leon, Guanajuato
Last Foreign Residence: Leon, Guanajuato
Married to: Juanita Ortega Solis   **Date:** Nov. 3, 1928
Where: Topeka, Kansas (Juanita was born in Iola, Kansas, on Aug. 27, 1912.)   **Crossed the Border on:** March 19, 1926
Where: El Paso, Texas   **Mode of travel:** El Paso Electric Railway   **Date Certificate Issued:** N.A.
Alien Registration: N.A.
Description: Occupation: Laborer. Dark Complexion, 5 Feet, 8 Inches, Dark Brown Eyes, Black Hair. Three children listed – born between 1929 and 1933.

NATURALIZATION EXTRACTS

Name: Jose Maria Soliz
District Court: County Court, County of Webb, Laredo, Texas **Address:** N.A.
Type of Record: Declaration of Intention, No. #1929
DOB: N.A. (23 years old) **Place:** Lampazos, Nuevo Leon
Last Foreign Residence: N.A.
Married to: N.A.   **Date:** N.A.
Where: N.A.
Crossed the Border on: May 10, 1882
Where: Laredo, Texas   **Mode of travel:** N.A.
Date Certificate Issued: October 27, 1886
Alien Registration: N.A.
Description: N.A.

NATURALIZATION EXTRACTS

Name: Charles Toribio Sommer
District Court: Superior Court, Cochise County, State of Arizona   **Address:** Box 802, Douglas, Arizona
Type of Record: Declaration of Intention, No. 956 (328658)   **DOB:** April 26, 1889   **Place:** Arivechi, Sahuapa, Sonora
Last Foreign Residence: Miua, Sonora
Married to: N.A.   **Date:** N.A.
Where: N.A.
Crossed the Border on: August 20, 1915
Where: Naco, Arizona   **Mode of travel:** Walked across   **Date Certificate Issued:** February 12, 1917 (Renounced allegiance to William II, German Emperor).   **Alien Registration:** N.A.
Description: Occupation: Auto Repairman. Dark Complexion, 5 Feet, 10 Inches, 143 Pounds, Dark Brown Hair, Brown Eyes.

NATURALIZATION EXTRACTS

Name: Fred Sommer
District Court: Superior Court, Cochise County, State of Arizona **Address:** Box 802, Douglas, Arizona
Type of Record: Declaration of Intention, No. 957 (328659) **DOB:** August 30, 1895   **Place:** Arivechi, Sonora
Last Foreign Residence: Miua, Sonora
Married to: N.A.   **Date:** N.A.
Where: N.A.
Crossed the Border on: September 22, 1915
Where: Douglas, Arizona   **Mode of travel:** Walked across
Date Certificate Issued: February 12, 1917 (Renounced allegiance to William II, German Emperor). **Alien Registration:** N.A.
Description: Occupation: Auto Repairman. Dark Complexion, 5 Feet, 10 Inches, 145 Pounds, Black Hair, Brown Eyes.

NATURALIZATION EXTRACTS

Name: Daniel Sotelo

District Court: District Court, Southern District of California, Los Angeles, California
Address: 10108 Graham Ave., Los Angeles, California

Type of Record: Declaration of Intention

DOB: Nov. 6, 1920   **Place:** Aguascalientes, Mexico

Last Foreign Residence: Aguascalientes, Mexico

Married to: Not married   **Date:** N.A.

Where: N.A.

Crossed the Border on: January 3, 1924

Where: El Paso, Texas   **Mode of travel:** El Paso Electric Railroad (Certificate of Arrival, No. 23-132628)
Date Certificate Issued: March 30, 1945

Alien Registration: N.A.

Description: Occupation: Vegetable Clerk. Light Complexion, 5 Feet, 2 Inches, Brown Eyes, Black Hair, 140 Pounds.

NATURALIZATION EXTRACTS

Name: Anastacio Sotero
District Court: District Court, Southern District of California, Los Angeles, California   **Address:** 726 Gibbons St., Los Angeles, California
Type of Record: Declaration of Intention, No. 133879
DOB: Feb. 15, 1906 **Place:** Santa Barbara, Mexico
Last Foreign Residence: Santa Barbara, Mexico
Married to: Eloisa **Date:** August 1, 1943
Where: Los Angeles, California (Eloisa was born in Durango, Mexico, on Jan. 12, 1910. She entered the U.S. at El Paso, Texas, on Aug. 23, 1916.)   **Crossed the Border on:** September 18, 1918
Where: El Paso, Texas **Mode of travel:** On foot (Certificate of Arrival, No. 23-103619)   **Date Certificate Issued:** March 12, 1945
Alien Registration: N.A.
Description: Occupation: Boiler Maker. Dark Complexion, 5 Feet, 5 Inches, Brown Eyes, Black Hair, 135 Pounds.

NATURALIZATION EXTRACTS

Name: Felix Soto
District Court: District Court, District of Colorado, Denver, Colorado   **Address:** 1511 West Evans Ave., Denver, Colorado
Type of Record: Declaration of Intention, No. 13454 (13640)   **DOB:** May 18, 1902   **Place:** Chihuahua, Mexico
Last Foreign Residence: Chihuahua, Mexico
Married to: Mary Soto   **Date:** October 21, 1921
Where: La Junta, Colorado (Mary was born at Chihuahua, Mexico, on January 9, 1905. She entered the U.S. on March 5, 1917 at El Paso, Texas.)   **Crossed the Border on:** August 7, 1915
Where: El Paso, Texas   **Mode of travel:** International Bridge (Certificate of Arrival, No. 18-8087)   **Date Certificate Issued:** December 13, 1939 (Previous Declaration of Intention made: No. 9494 on Feb. 4, 1925 at Denver, Colorado.)   **Alien Registration:** N.A.
Description: Occupation: Laborer. Dark complexion, 5 Feet, 10 Inches, 170 Pounds, Black Hair, Brown Eyes. Three children listed – all born between 1922 and 1925.

NATURALIZATION EXTRACTS

Name: Rudolph Soto aka Rudolfo Soto
District Court: District Court, District of Colorado, Denver, Colorado **Address:** 2737 Lawrence St., Denver, Colorado
Type of Record: Declaration of Intention, No. 13109
DOB: Sept. 20, 1907   **Place:** Chihuahua, Mexico
Last Foreign Residence: Chihuahua, Mexico
Married to: Not married   **Date:** N.A.
Where: N.A.
Crossed the Border on: July 1, 1908 (Crossed under the name of Rudolfo Soto) **Where:** El Paso, Texas   **Mode of travel:** International Bridge (Certificate of Arrival, No. 18-7792) **Date Certificate Issued:** August 4, 1938
Alien Registration: N.A.
Description: Occupation: Clerk – fruit stand. Dark complexion, 5 Feet, 9½ Inches, 141 Pounds, Black Hair, Brown Eyes.

NATURALIZATION EXTRACTS

Name: Carolina Torres
District Court: District Court, District of Colorado, Denver, Colorado **Address:** 2497 19th St., Denver, Colorado
Type of Record: Declaration of Intention, No. 13962
DOB: Oct. 26, 1918   **Place:** Chihuahua, Chihuahua
Last Foreign Residence: Chihuahua, Mexico
Married to: Not married   **Date:** N.A.
Where: N.A.
Crossed the Border on: Jan. 15, 1920
Where: El Paso, Texas   **Mode of travel:** El Paso Electric Railway (Certificate of Arrival, No. 19-11355) **Date Certificate Issued:** April 29, 1941
Alien Registration: N.A.
Description: Occupation: Housework. Dark complexion, 5 Feet, 1 Inches, Black Hair, Brown Eyes.

NATURALIZATION EXTRACTS

Name: Onesino Torres
District Court: District Court, District of Colorado, Denver, Colorado   **Address:** 1129 5th Street, Denver, Colorado
Type of Record: Declaration of Intention, No. 13229 (18275)   **DOB:** Oct. 5, 1894   **Place:** San Antonio, San Luis Potosi
Last Foreign Residence: Torreon, Coahuila
Married to: Maria Torres Salon   **Date:** May 15, 1915
Where: Torreon, Coahuila (Maria was born at Tapachula, Chiapas, on May 14, 1895. She entered the U.S. at El Paso, Texas, on August 12, 1916.)   **Crossed the Border on:** August 12, 1916
Where: El Paso, Texas   **Mode of travel:** International Bridge (Certificate of Arrival, No. 19-7252)   **Date Certificate Issued:** February 20, 1939
Alien Registration: N.A.
Description: Occupation: Laborer. Dark complexion, 5 Feet, 4 Inches, 125 Pounds, Black Hair, Brown Eyes. Seven children listed – all born between 1916 and 1937.

NATURALIZATION EXTRACTS

Name: Jose Jesus Trejo	
District Court: District Court, Los Angeles, California	
Address: 232 S. Ave. 18, Los Angeles, California	
Type of Record: Petition for Naturalization, No. 68566 (470812) **DOB:** Jan. 14, 1903 **Place:** Zacatecas, Mexico	
Last Foreign Residence: Torreon, Coahuila	
Married to: Silvia **Date:** July 16, 1932	
Where: Los Angeles, California (Silvia was born in Congress, Arizona, on Dec. 31, 1903.) **Crossed the Border on:** September 6, 1918	
Where: El Paso, Texas **Mode of travel:** El Paso Electric Railway (Certificate of Arrival, No. 23-71094) **Date Certificate Issued:** October 3, 1939	
Alien Registration: N.A.	
Description: Occupation: Janitor.	

NATURALIZATION EXTRACTS

Name: Antonio Trevino
District Court: County Court, County of Webb, Laredo, Texas **Address:** N.A.
Type of Record: Declaration of Intention
DOB: N.A. (40 years old) **Place:** Cadereyta, Nuevo Leon
Last Foreign Residence: N.A.
Married to: N.A.   **Date:** N.A.
Where: N.A.
Crossed the Border on: November 15, 1869
Where: Davis, Texas **Mode of travel:** N.A.
Date Certificate Issued: November 7, 1892
Alien Registration: N.A.
Description: N.A.

NATURALIZATION EXTRACTS

Name: Edmundo Antonio Trevino
District Court: District Court, Southern District of California, Los Angeles, California   **Address:** 1513 W. 58th St., Los Angeles, California
Type of Record: Declaration of Intention
DOB: Jan. 17, 1901   **Place:** Piedras Negras, Coahuila
Last Foreign Residence: Piedras Negras, Coahuila
Married to: Celia   **Date:** Oct. 14, 1926
Where: San Pedro, California (Celia was born at Guaymas, Sonora, on March 25, 1904. She entered the U.S. at El Paso, Texas, on January 1, 1920.)   **Crossed the Border on:** May 21, 1907
Where: Eagle Pass, Texas   **Mode of travel:** Toll bridge (Certificate of Arrival, No. 23-x-22715)   **Date Certificate Issued:** March 28, 1945
Alien Registration: N.A.
Description: Occupation: Railroad Clerk. Light Complexion, 5 Feet, 11 Inches, Brown Eyes, Black Hair, 136 Pounds.

NATURALIZATION EXTRACTS

Name: Melchor Trevino
District Court: District Court, District of Colorado, Denver, Colorado **Address:** 2132 Larimer St., Denver, Colorado
Type of Record: Declaration of Intention, No. 13955
DOB: Jan. 6, 1882　　**Place:** Villa Garcia, Nuevo Leon
Last Foreign Residence: Juarez, Chihuahua
Married to: Not married　　　　**Date:** N.A.
Where: N.A.
Crossed the Border on: Oct. 23, 1920
Where: El Paso, Texas　　**Mode of travel:** El Paso Electric Railway (Certificate of Arrival, No. 19-11041) **Date Certificate Issued:** April 22, 1941
Alien Registration: N.A.
Description: Occupation: Pool Hall owner. Dark complexion, 5 Feet, 6 Inches, 160 Pounds, Black Hair, Brown Eyes.

NATURALIZATION EXTRACTS

Name: Serapio Trevino
District Court: County Court, County of Maverick, Eagle Pass, Texas
Address: N.A.
Type of Record: Declaration of Intention
DOB: N.A. (25 years old) **Place:** Monterrey, Nuevo Leon
Last Foreign Residence: N.A.
Married to: N.A.   **Date:** N.A.
Where: N.A.
Crossed the Border on: July 1883
Where: Eagle Pass, Texas   **Mode of travel:** N.A.
Date Certificate Issued: November 3, 1884
Alien Registration: N.A.
Description: N.A.

NATURALIZATION EXTRACTS

Name: Francisco Vallejo Valdez aka Joseph Vallejo Costello
District Court: District Court, Southern District of California, Los Angeles, California
Address: 1142 Santee St., Los Angeles, California
Type of Record: Declaration of Intention, No. 123844
DOB: Oct. 4, 1901   **Place:** Sierra Mojada, Coahuila
Last Foreign Residence: Jimenez, Chihuahua
Married to: N.A.   **Date:** N.A.
Where: N.A.
Crossed the Border on: November 11, 1918 (Crossed under the name of Francisco Vallejo Valdez)
Where: El Paso, Texas   **Mode of travel:** On foot (Certificate of Arrival, No. 23-82935)
Date Certificate Issued: March 8, 1945 (Declaration of Intention signed on October 13, 1919 in San Francisco, California.)
Alien Registration: N.A.
Description: Occupation: Mech. Painter. Dark Complexion, 5 Feet, 7½ Inches, Brown Eyes, Dark Brown Hair, 132 Pounds.

NATURALIZATION EXTRACTS

Name: Jesus Valdez
District Court: County Court, County of Webb, Laredo, Texas
Address: N.A.
Type of Record: Declaration of Intention
DOB: N.A. (22 years old) **Place:** Cerralvo, Nuevo Leon
Last Foreign Residence: N.A.
Married to: N.A.   **Date:** N.A.
Where: N.A.
Crossed the Border on: September 16, 1888
Where: Laredo, Texas   **Mode of travel:** N.A.
Date Certificate Issued: November 1, 1890
Alien Registration: N.A.
Description: N.A.

NATURALIZATION EXTRACTS

Name: Jesus Valle
District Court: County Court, County of Webb, Laredo, Texas
Address: N.A.
Type of Record: Declaration of Intention, No. #1902
DOB: N.A. (37 years old) **Place:** Sabinas Hidalgo, Nuevo Leon
Last Foreign Residence: N.A.
Married to: N.A. **Date:** N.A.
Where: N.A.
Crossed the Border on: October 15, 1875
Where: Laredo, Texas **Mode of travel:** N.A.
Date Certificate Issued: October 30, 1886
Alien Registration: N.A.
Description: N.A.

NATURALIZATION EXTRACTS

Name: Cristobal Vallejo
District Court: County Court, County of Webb, Laredo, Texas **Address:** N.A.
Type of Record: Declaration of Intention
DOB: N.A. (22 years old) **Place:** Monterrey, Nuevo Leon
Last Foreign Residence: N.A.
Married to: N.A.   **Date:** N.A.
Where: N.A.
Crossed the Border on: June 15, 1881
Where: Laredo, Texas **Mode of travel:** N.A.
Date Certificate Issued: November 5, 1892
Alien Registration: N.A.
Description: N.A.

NATURALIZATION EXTRACTS

Name: Inez Vargas aka Agnes Vargas (Sister Olga)
District Court: District Court, District of Colorado, Denver, Colorado
Address: St. Anthony's Hospital, Denver, Colorado
Type of Record: Declaration of Intention, No. 13291 (18424)
DOB: Jan. 21, 1916 **Place:** Villa Morelos, Michoacan
Last Foreign Residence: Villa Morelos, Michoacan
Married to: Not married   **Date:** N.A.
Where: N.A.
Crossed the Border on: Oct. 28, 1918 (Crossed under the name of Inez Vargas)
Where: El Paso, Texas   **Mode of travel:** El Paso Electric Railway (Certificate of Arrival, No. 9-18462)
Date Certificate Issued: May 23, 1939
Alien Registration: N.A.
Description: Occupation: Domestic. Dark complexion, 5 Feet, 6 Inches, 162 Pounds, Black Hair, Brown Eyes.

NATURALIZATION EXTRACTS

Name: Rosario Vargas
District Court: District Court, Southern District of California, Los Angeles, California   **Address:** 1852 Middleton Place, Los Angeles, California
Type of Record: Declaration of Intention, No. 123849
DOB: Sept. 2, 1922   **Place:** Irapuato, Guanajuato
Last Foreign Residence: Irapuato, Guanajuato
Married to: N.A.   **Date:** N.A.
Where: N.A.
Crossed the Border on: August 4, 1924 (Crossed under the name of Maria Vargas)   **Where:** El Paso, Texas   **Mode of travel:** El Paso Electric Railroad (Certificate of Arrival, No. 23-132270)   **Date Certificate Issued:** March 9, 1945
Alien Registration: N.A.
Description: Occupation: Secretary. Light Complexion, 5 Feet, 1¾ Inches, Brown Eyes, Dark Brown Hair, 112 Pounds.

NATURALIZATION EXTRACTS

Name: Francisco Vasquez aka Frank Garcia Vasquez
District Court: District Court, District of Colorado, Denver, Colorado **Address:** 3213 Curtis St., Denver, Colorado
Type of Record: Declaration of Intention, No. 14607
DOB: April 10, 1905   **Place:** Concepcion del Oro, Zacatecas **Last Foreign Residence:** Concepcion del Oro, Zacatecas
Married to: Nicolasa Magellan   **Date:** Dec. 2, 1937
Where: Greeley, Colorado. (Nicolasa was born on Sept. 10, 1913 at La Barca, Jalisco. She entered the U.S. at Laredo, Texas, on Sept. 14, 1928.) **Crossed the Border on:** Aug. 30, 1916 (Crossed under the name of Francisco Vasquez) **Where:** Laredo, Texas   **Mode of travel:** Footbridge (Certificate of Arrival, No. 18-14185) **Date Certificate Issued:** February 10, 1945
Alien Registration: N.A.
Description: Occupation: Laborer. Dark complexion, 5 Feet, 4 Inches, 120 Pounds, Black Hair, Brown Eyes. Three children listed – all born between 1928 and 1934.

NATURALIZATION EXTRACTS

Name: Roberto Manuel Vasquez
District Court: District Court, Southern District of California, Los Angeles, California **Address:** 1331 W. 30th St., Los Angeles, California
Type of Record: Declaration of Intention
DOB: Feb. 26, 1911 **Place:** Santa Barbara, Chihuahua
Last Foreign Residence: Parral, Chihuahua
Married to: Maria **Date:** August 26, 1941
Where: Parral, Chihuahua (Maria was born in Parral, Chihuahua, on Sept. 11, 1918. She entered the U.S. at El Paso, Texas, on Oct. 3, 1944.) **Crossed the Border on:** October 3, 1944
Where: El Paso, Texas **Mode of travel:** El Paso City Lines, Inc. (Certificate of Arrival, No. 23-133126) **Date Certificate Issued:** June 9, 1945
Alien Registration: N.A.
Description: Occupation: Electrician. Dark Complexion, Brown Eyes, Black Hair, 5 Feet, 6 Inches, 160 Pounds.

NATURALIZATION EXTRACTS

Name: Teofilo Velasco
District Court: District Court, Los Angeles, California
Address: 634 Maplewood Ave. Bellflower, California
Type of Record: Petition for Naturalization, No. 472262
DOB: Dec. 18, 1910   **Place:** Guadalajara, Jalisco
Last Foreign Residence: Guadalajara, Jalisco
Married to: Esperanza   **Date:** April 26, 1936
Where: Los Angeles, California (Esperanza was born in Amarillo, Texas, on Nov, 4, 1915.) **Crossed the Border on:** April 10, 1928
Where: El Paso, Texas   **Mode of travel:** El Paso Electric Railway (Certificate of Arrival, No. 23-69824) **Date Certificate Issued:** September 25, 1939
Alien Registration: N.A.
Description: Occupation: Milker. One Child listed – born in 1936.

NATURALIZATION EXTRACTS

Name: Jesus Velasquez
District Court: District Court, District of Colorado, Denver, Colorado
Address: 405 Genesio St., Lafayette, Boulder County, Colorado
Type of Record: Declaration of Intention, No. 12793 (17595)
DOB: April 13, 1900   **Place:** Teocaltiche, Jalisco
Last Foreign Residence: Teocaltiche, Jalisco
Married to: Frances Velasquez   **Date:** Sept. 28, 1925
Where: Lafayette, Colorado (Frances was born at Walsenburg, Colorado, on August 9, 1906.)
Crossed the Border on: May 6, 1916
Where: El Paso, Texas   **Mode of travel:** El Paso Electric Railway (Certificate of Arrival, No. 18-10535)
Date Certificate Issued: May 14, 1937
Alien Registration: N.A.
Description: Occupation: Coal mining. Dark complexion, 5 Feet, 6 Inches, 145 Pounds, Dark Brown Hair, Brown Eyes. One child listed – born in 1926.

NATURALIZATION EXTRACTS

Name: Asencion Velez
District Court: County Court, County of Webb, Laredo, Texas **Address:** N.A.
Type of Record: Declaration of Intention
DOB: N.A. (21 years old) **Place:** Saltillo, Coahuila
Last Foreign Residence: N.A.
Married to: N.A.　　**Date:** N.A.
Where: N.A.
Crossed the Border on: November 1898
Where: Laredo, Texas **Mode of travel:** N.A.
Date Certificate Issued: January 31, 1906
Alien Registration: N.A.
Description: N.A.

NATURALIZATION EXTRACTS

Name: Rosa Villavicencio Venegas
District Court: District Court, Southern District of California, Los Angeles, California **Address:** 1515 Hancock St., Los Angeles, California
Type of Record: Declaration of Intention
DOB: Sept. 4, 1879 **Place:** Huejucar, Jalisco
Last Foreign Residence: Parral, Chihuahua
Married to: Albino **Date:** May 25, 1935
Where: Hidalgo, Mexico (Albino was born at Huejucar, Jalisco, date unknown. He entered the U.S. at San Francisco, California, date unknown.)
Crossed the Border on: September 25, 1919 (Crossed the border under the name of Rosa Villavicancio de Venegas)
Where: El Paso, Texas **Mode of travel:** El Paso Electric Railroad (Certificate of Arrival, No. 23-133478)
Date Certificate Issued: July 13, 1945
Alien Registration: N.A.
Description: Occupation: Photographer. Medium Complexion, 5 Feet, 3 Inches, 165 Pounds, Brown Hair, Brown Eyes. One child listed – born in 1907.

NATURALIZATION EXTRACTS

Name: Julio C. Verdin
District Court: District Court, Ft. Scott, Kansas
Address: 908 S. Steuben Ave. Chanute, Neosho County, Kansas **Type of Record:** Declaration of Intention
DOB: Feb. 16, 1882   **Place:** Encarnacion de Diaz, Jalisco
Last Foreign Residence: Aguascalientes, Mexico
Married to: Felicitas Verdin   **Date:** Sept. 20, 1901
Where: Aguascalientes, Mexico (Felicitas was born at Aguascalientes, Mexico, on May 18, 1880. She entered the U.S. at El Paso, Texas, on April 24, 1908.) **Crossed the Border on:** May 5, 1907 (Crossed the border under the name of Julio Cortez Verdin) **Where:** El Paso, Texas   **Mode of travel:** Electric Railway (Certificate of Arrival, No. 16-R11830) **Date Certificate Issued:** March 19, 1944
Alien Registration: N.A.
Description: Occupation: Railroad Boilermaker. Light Complexion, Brown Eyes, Black Hair, 5 Feet, 4 Inches, 120 Pounds. Three children listed – all born between 1909 and 1918.

NATURALIZATION EXTRACTS

Name: Alejandro Verdines	
District Court: District Court, Los Angeles, California	
Address: 716 N. Bonnie Beach Place, Los Angeles, California	
Type of Record: Petition for Naturalization, No. 68422 (472430)	
DOB: Nov. 26, 1882	**Place:** Mazatlan, Sinaloa
Last Foreign Residence: Nogales, Sonora	
Married to: Antonia	**Date:** January 12, 1939
Where: Garden Grove, California (Antonia was born in El Paso, Texas, on June 13, 1886.)	
Crossed the Border on: July 5, 1923	
Where: Nogales, Arizona (Certificate of Arrival, No. 23-70522)	**Mode of travel:** Afoot
Date Certificate Issued: September 29, 1939	
Alien Registration: N.A.	
Description: Occupation: Truck drive, plumber and electrician.	

NATURALIZATION EXTRACTS

Name: Jose Ramirez Villanueva

District Court: District Court, Southern District of California, Los Angeles, California
Address: 202 N. Eastinal, Los Angeles, California

Type of Record: Declaration of Intention

DOB: July 19, 1902 **Place:** Santa Barbara, Chihuahua

Last Foreign Residence: Santa Barbara, Chihuahua

Married to: Concha **Date:** April 19, 1923

Where: El Paso, Texas (Concha was born in Casas Grandes, Chihuahua, on April 11, 1901. She entered the U.S. at El Paso, Texas, on Aug. 15, 1906.)
Crossed the Border on: August 10, 1921

Where: El Paso, Texas **Mode of travel:** El Paso Electric Railway (Certificate of Arrival, No. 23-133213)
Date Certificate Issued: June 9, 1945

Alien Registration: N.A.

Description: Occupation: Tools and Machinery. Dark Complexion, Brown Eyes, Black Hair, 5 Feet, 8 Inches, 171 Pounds. Two children listed – born in 1926 and 1929.

NATURALIZATION EXTRACTS

Name: Santos Villareal
District Court: County Court, County of Maverick, Eagle Pass, Texas **Address:** N.A.
Type of Record: Declaration of Intention
DOB: N.A. (24 years old)　　**Place:** Mexico City, Mexico
Last Foreign Residence: N.A.
Married to: N.A.　　**Date:** N.A.
Where: N.A.
Crossed the Border on: July 22, 1871
Where: Eagle Pass, Texas　**Mode of travel:** N.A.
Date Certificate Issued: October 19, 1886
Alien Registration: N.A.
Description: N.A.

NATURALIZATION EXTRACTS

Name: Valentin Villegas
District Court: County Court, County of Webb, Laredo, Texas **Address:** N.A.
Type of Record: Declaration of Intention
DOB: N.A. (31 years old) **Place:** Guerrero, Tamaulipas
Last Foreign Residence: N.A.
Married to: N.A. **Date:** N.A.
Where: N.A.
Crossed the Border on: June 9, 1906
Where: Carrizo, Texas **Mode of travel:** N.A.
Date Certificate Issued: June 9, 1906
Alien Registration: N.A.
Description: N.A.

NATURALIZATION EXTRACTS

Name: Encarnacion Ybarra
District Court: County Court, County of Webb, Laredo, Texas **Address:** N.A.
Type of Record: Declaration of Intention, No. #1919
DOB: N.A. (25 years old) **Place:** Saltillo, Coahuila
Last Foreign Residence: N.A.
Married to: N.A.   **Date:** N.A.
Where: N.A.
Crossed the Border on: February 14, 1878
Where: Laredo, Texas **Mode of travel:** N.A.
Date Certificate Issued: October 28, 1886
Alien Registration: N.A.
Description: N.A.

NATURALIZATION EXTRACTS

Name: Lorenzo Yglecias

District Court: County Court, County of Maverick, Eagle Pass, Texas

Address: N.A.

Type of Record: Declaration of Intention

DOB: N.A. (45 years old)   **Place:** Zaragoza, Coahuila

Last Foreign Residence: N.A.

Married to: N.A.   **Date:** N.A.

Where: N.A.

Crossed the Border on: Summer 1884

Where: Eagle Pass, Texas   **Mode of travel:** N.A.

Date Certificate Issued: November 5, 1892

Alien Registration: N.A.

Description: N.A.

NATURALIZATION EXTRACTS

Name: Fernando Yrungarai
District Court: Superior Court, Cochise County, State of Arizona **Address:** Bisbee, Arizona
Type of Record: Declaration of Intention
DOB: May 30, 1887 **Place:** Abino, Durango
Last Foreign Residence: Abino, Durango
Married to: N.A. **Date:** N.A.
Where: N.A.
Crossed the Border on: February 29, 1908
Where: El Paso, Texas **Mode of travel:** Mexican Central Railroad **Date Certificate Issued:** December 9, 1914
Alien Registration: N.A.
Description: Occupation: Laborer. Dark Complexion, 5 Feet, 6 Inches, 150 Pounds, Black Hair, Brown Eyes.

NATURALIZATION EXTRACTS

Name: Gilberto Zabala aka Gilberto Zabala Bocanegra
District Court: District Court, Los Angeles, California
Address: 416 E. 42nd Place, Los Angeles, California (2406 S. Trinity St., Los Angeles in the Declaration of Intention) **Type of Record:** Petition for Naturalization, No. 70823 (695755) **DOB:** July 18, 1900 **Place:** Torreon, Coahuila
Last Foreign Residence: Torreon, Coahuila
Married to: Soledad   **Date:** September 7, 1926
Where: Los Angeles, California (Soledad was born at Parral, Chihuahua, on Sept. 16, 1889. She entered the U.S. at El Paso, Texas, on Sept. 18, 1924.)
Crossed the Border on: July 3, 1922 (Crossed under the name of Gilberto Bocanegra)
Where: El Paso, Texas **Mode of travel:** El Paso Electric Railway (Certificate of Arrival, No. 23-38994)
Date Certificate Issued: January 2, 1940 (Declaration of Intention No. 76153 (13558) filed on June 13, 1936 in District Court, Los Angeles.)
Alien Registration: N.A.
Description: Occupation: Handyman. Light Complexion, Brown Eyes, Black Hair, 5 Feet, 4 Inches, 149 Pounds.

NATURALIZATION EXTRACTS

Name: Amelia Zanka
District Court: District Court, Los Angeles, California
Address: 725 Stanford St., Los Angeles, California
Type of Record: Petition for Naturalization, No. 74109 (696286)
DOB: July 7, 1901 **Place:** Sierra Mojada, Coahuila
Last Foreign Residence: Parral, Chihuahua
Married to: Antonino Zanka **Date:** April 29, 1943
Where: Los Angeles, California (Antonino was born at Filicudi, Italy, on Nov. 19, 1892. He entered the U.S. at Boston, Massachusetts, in October 1906.) **Crossed the Border on:** September 10, 1906
Where: El Paso, Texas **Mode of travel:** Street car (Certificate of Arrival, No. 23R63569) **Date Certificate Issued:** January 15, 1940
Alien Registration: N.A.
Description: Occupation: Janitress. One child listed – born in 1924. Husband Antonino Zanka was naturalized on Nov. 20, 1918 at Superior Court in San Diego, California.

NATURALIZATION EXTRACTS

Name: Octaviano Zapata
District Court: County Court, County of Maverick, Eagle Pass, Texas **Address:** N.A.
Type of Record: Declaration of Intention
DOB: N.A. (22 years old) **Place:** Piedras Negras, Coahuila **Last Foreign Residence:** N.A.
Married to: N.A. **Date:** N.A.
Where: N.A.
Crossed the Border on: September 18, 1883
Where: Eagle Pass, Texas **Mode of travel:** N.A.
Date Certificate Issued: October 16, 1886
Alien Registration: N.A.
Description: N.A.

NATURALIZATION EXTRACTS

Name: Pedro Zaragosa aka Pete Zaragoza
District Court: U.S. District Court, Fort Scott, Kansas
Address: 1203 N. Steuben, Chanut County, Kansas
Type of Record: Declaration of Intention
DOB: June 29, 1906 **Place:** Silas, Mexico
Last Foreign Residence: Juarez, Chihuahua
Married to: Susana Guerra **Date:** June 3, 1934
Where: Chanute, Kansas (Susana was born at Puruandiro, Michoacan, on May 24, 1910. She entered the U.S. at Laredo, Texas, in 1912.)
Crossed the Border on: March 16, 1917 (Crossed under the name of Pedro Zaragoza)
Where: El Paso, Texas **Mode of travel:** El Paso Electric Railway (Certificate of Arrival, No. 16-11082)
Date Certificate Issued: October 2, 1941 Departed the U.S. at Laredo on Jan. 11, 1938; returned to the U.S. at Laredo on Jan. 15, 1938.
Alien Registration: N.A.
Description: Occupation: Sack-Tyer. Cement Plan. Dark Complexion, Brown Eyes, Black Hair, 5 Feet, 5 Inches, 160 Pounds. Five children listed – all born between 1928 and 1940.

BIBLIOGRAPHY

National Archives and Regional Administration (NARA), *Index to Naturalization Records of the U.S. District Court for the Southern District of California, Central Division, Los Angeles, 1887-1937* [NARA M1607].

NARA, *Naturalization Index Cards of the United States District Court for the Southern District of California, Central Division, Los Angeles, 1915-1976* [NARA M1525].

NARA, *Naturalization Records of the United States District Court for the Southern District of California, Central Division, Los Angeles, 1887-1940* [NARA M1524].

NARA, *Naturalization Records of the United States District Court for the Territory of Arizona* [NARA M1616 and NARA M1615].

NARA, *Naturalization Records Created by the U.S. District Court in Colorado, 1877-1952* [NARA M1192].

BIBLIOGRAPHY

Texas. District Court (Maverick County). *Record of Declarations (1882-1906)* [Family History Film #1016784].

Texas. County Court (Webb County). *Records of Declarations, 1886-1907* [Family History Film #1017220].

United States. District Court (Kansas: First Division), *Microfilm of Originals in the National Archives Branch in Kansas City, Missouri. Declarations of intention, 1908-1942; Naturalizations, 1865-1984* [Family History Films #1711262 to 1711266, and 1728345 to 1728347].

INDEX

297

Other books by John P. Schmal:

Naturalizations of Mexican Americans: Extracts
Volumes 1-4

The Journey to Latino Political Representation

Mexican-American Genealogical Research:
Following the Paper Trail to Mexico
Donna S. Morales and John P. Schmal

The Indigenous Roots of a Mexican-American Family
Donna S. Morales and John P. Schmal

The Dominguez Family: A Mexican-American Journey
Donna S. Morales and John P. Schmal

A Mexican-American Family of California:
In the Service of Three Flags
John P. Schmal and Jennifer Vo